Luis De la Palma

A Treatise on the Particular Examen of Conscience According to the Method of St. Ignatius

Luis De la Palma
A Treatise on the Particular Examen of Conscience According to the Method of St. Ignatius
ISBN/EAN: 9783744659994

Printed in Europe, USA, Canada, Australia, Japan

Cover: Foto ©ninafisch / pixelio.de

More available books at **www.hansebooks.com**

ST. JOSEPH'S ASCETICAL LIBRARY.

EDITED BY FATHERS S.J.

No. VII.

A TREATISE ON THE PARTICULAR EXAMEN OF CONSCIENCE.

ROEHAMPTON:
PRINTED BY JAMES STANLEY.

A TREATISE

ON THE

Particular Examen of Conscience,

ACCORDING TO THE METHOD

OF

ST. IGNATIUS.

BY

FATHER LUIS DE LA PALMA,

Of the Society of Jesus.

AUTHOR OF THE "HISTORY OF THE SACRED PASSION."

With Preface by

FATHER GEORGE PORTER, S.J.

LONDON: BURNS AND OATES.

1873.

PREFACE.

THE *Treatise on the Particular Examen of Conscience*, by Father Luis de la Palma, of the Society of Jesus, fully explains the nature and the use of this Spiritual Exercise, as it was taught by St. Ignatius in his book of the Exercises.

Since the time of St. Ignatius, the Particular Examen has been adopted to a considerable extent, both by Religious and by persons in the world, aspiring to perfection, and, very generally, by the active Orders which have sprung up since the time of the first French Revolution.

It was to be expected that the nature and true object of the Particular Examen would be often misunderstood, and sometimes, the name was given to an Exercise, as unlike the Particular Examen of St. Ignatius as anything that could be imagined.

Instances are not wanting, in which Religious, making the General Examination of Conscience at midday and in the evening, were instructed to write down all the faults of the morning and the afternoon, and taught to consider such noting down as the Particular Examen.

A more frequent mistake in the use of the Particular Examen is the attempting to cover too much ground. How often are Novices found who make Humility the subject of their Particular Examen, or Conformity to the will of God, or Charity? It is of the very essence of the Particular Examen, that the subject-matter should be limited and narrowed and made as definite as possible. Not Humility in general, but Humility in action or in word, and that under some well-defined circumstances, *v.g.*, in word, in speaking to one's equals, or to one particular person; not Conformity to the will of God in general, but Conformity to the will of God in the matter of health, or in one's occupations, or in one's Superiors; not Charity in general, but Charity towards such a one, in word, never blaming him or finding fault with him—these are fitting subjects for the Particular Examen.

Humility in general, or Conformity in general, or Charity in general, are as little suited for the subject of the Particular Examen as Christianity in general or Virtue in general. The efficacy of the Particular Examen lies in the selection of a definite, limited object, and in the exercise of watchfulness over self, self-examination, constancy in purpose, frequent renewal of one's resolution on this definite object. Happy should we be if we could extend to the whole field of our daily spiritual life this care and thought, but human nature is not capable of bearing such a strain, and therefore it is only attempted where it can be easily endured.

For the same reason, experienced masters in spiritual life teach us to select for the Particular Examen such acts of virtue or such faults as may be seen outwardly. Merely internal acts more easily escape notice, and the soul is harassed in endeavouring to follow them. Advancement in virtue is rendered more easy when the attention is directed to the outward action, and it is traced up to its source and origin.

To make this subdivision more intelligible we will subjoin some examples, taken from Nepveu's *Spirit of Christianity* (*vide* Appendix, p. 133).

Lastly, a word may be addressed to that large body of pious persons who shrink from the use of the Particular Examen, complain that it is irksome, and say that they find no matter on which to exercise it. Those who speak thus are for the most part persons of a good natural disposition, of an even temperament, freed from any dangerous external temptations, and not tried by any very arduous duties. They feel no special attraction to fight their way to exalted perfection; they avoid any deliberate faults; their days are filled by a succession of duties, and they hope to end their lives in the same smooth and tranquil course.

It cannot be denied that there are, especially in inclosed Orders, many whose natural dispositions, innocence of lives, and habits of industry, protect them from serious dangers, and render Religious life sweet and easy to them. They encounter no particular difficulties, they are not exposed to any particular trials, they may, without peril to their perseverance, leave on one side this Exercise of the Particular Examen, or any other corresponding to it. But those whose vocation engages them in the active service of their neighbours, who may expect to see their Superiors frequently changed, who may be removed themselves from place to place, from one duty to another, who are tempted by so many distractions, and surrounded by so many occasions of sin, who, in one word, are called to live in the world and not be of the world, must aspire to solid virtues, virtues deeply rooted in the understanding and in the heart, virtues strengthened by habits of self-examination and strict discipline, virtues, in fine, acquired either by the Particular Examen or some similar spiritual exercise. Virtues which rest on a less solid foundation, which appear to be strong till they are put to the test, virtues which survive as long as everything around us favours goodness, virtues which are found wanting in the first shock of real temptation, will not carry the Religious of active Orders through the difficulties of their calling. Here is the secret of many wretched apostacies, of vocations abandoned, of falling away from first fervour, of the prime of life—perhaps of old age—wasted in tepidity and uselessness. The cost of the spiritual edifice had not been carefully calculated ; the foundations were not laid deep and broad ; the irksomeness of constant vigilance, of unceasing efforts to bring the natural man into subjection to the spiritual man, was thought too great: and "the rain fell, and the floods came, and the winds blew, and they beat upon that house, and it fell, and great was the ruin thereof."* *Tantum proficies quantum tibi ipse vim intuleris*†—"In proportion as thou dost violence to thyself, the greater progress wilt thou make." Or as St. Ignatius

---

* St. Matt. vii. 27. † *Imit. Christi*, cap. xxv., n. 11.

expresses the same in his book of the Exercises,* "Let every one reflect that he will make progress in spiritual life, in proportion as he divests himself of self-love, of self-will, and of self-interest"—*Cogitet enim unusquisque, tantum se profectum facturum esse in omnibus rebus spiritualibus, quantum exiverit a proprio suo amore, a propria voluntate et commoditate propria.*

* Hebd. ii., De Reformatione Vitæ. Versio autog.

CONTENTS.

	Page
PREFACE	v

Chap.

		Page
I.	What the Particular Examen consists in. Its difficulties	1
II.	From what causes the neglect of this Examen arises	10
III.	The form or method of this Examen, beginning with the resolve to be made on rising . . .	19
IV.	On the qualities requisite for a good purpose . .	34
V.	Of two other qualities of a good resolution . .	40
VI.	Of the care we are to take to put our morning resolution into practice	45
VII.	Of the times of this Examen, and the four additions concerning it	56
VIII.	The efficacy of this Examen	62
IX.	The matter of the Particular Examen . . .	69
X.	Reply to certain objections to the above . .	75
XI.	The manner and order of choosing the matter of the Particular Examen	81
XII.	Further instructions on the same subject . .	86
XIII.	Examples of each vice to illustrate the division of the Examen	90

CONTENTS.

Chap.		Page
XIV.	Of the subject-matter of the Particular Examen for such as are troubled with no vice in particular	100
XV.	The matter of the Particular Examen for beginners	102
XVI.	The matter of the Particular Examen for proficients	108
XVII.	The matter of the Particular Examen for the perfect	113
XVIII.	Formula of certain meditations helping on this Examen	115
XIX.	The end of this Examen	122
XX.	For whom is this Examen suited?	128

APPENDIX.

Defects contrary to humility	133
Defects contrary to meekness	135
Various acts of contempt of the world	137
Various acts of mortification	139

TREATISE ON THE PARTICULAR EXAMEN OF CONSCIENCE.

CHAPTER I.

WHAT THE PARTICULAR EXAMEN CONSISTS IN.
ITS DIFFICULTIES.

OUR holy Father St. Ignatius explains the Particular Examen at the commencement of the Book of Exercises in the following words—

The Particular and daily Examen, comprising three times, adapted to rightly disposing ourselves, and including a twofold examination.

The first time is in the morning, when one, immediately on rising from rest, should resolve to watch himself in regard of some sin, or special particular fault, of which he wishes to cure himself.

The second time is at noon, when one must ask grace from God to remember the number of times into which he has fallen into that sin or particular fault, and to guard against it for the future. Then he makes his first examination, requiring an account

2   What the Particular Examen consists in.

from his soul regarding the said sin or fault, how often he has committed it through the several parts of the day from the hour of rising down to the hour of this exercise: afterwards he marks as many points in the uppermost line of the annexed table. This being done, he once more resolves to guard himself with greater diligence through the remainder of the day.

The third time is at night, after supper; the second examination ought to be made through the several hours of the day, from the former examination down to the present; and in the same manner, having recalled and counted the number of times one has fallen, he will make an equal number of marks on the second line of a table like the annexed one prepared for the purpose—

D ──────────────

d ────────────

d ────────────

d ──────────

d ─────────

d ────────

d ──────

Though we find some maxims respecting such an Examen in the holy Fathers, and even in the Pagan philosophers, no one ever propounded this practice under the name of the Particular Examen, and no one ever suggested the observations made by St. Ignatius. Hence the Particular Examen may be considered as peculiar to the Society, and we may believe it was suggested to her Founder by the Holy Ghost, Who is believed to have dictated the Constitutions, and inspired the Exercises as a means to the perfect observance of the Constitutions.

Following the footsteps of our holy Founder, we may define, or rather describe, the Particular Examen in the following manner—

The Particular Examen is a spiritual contest against some particular fault, and comprises a purpose not to fall, an anxious desire to keep this purpose, an examination whether we have fallen, and a comparison between different intervals (times), that we may discover whether any correction has been obtained, and to what extent, and that in this manner the fault which most hinders us may be thoroughly uprooted, and the virtue we stand in need of be implanted in our hearts.

This exercise is suited to every description of persons, and to all seasons and times.

The preceding description gives us the nature of the Particular Examen: it is a spiritual struggle or contest; and it assigns the causes of the exercise, the material cause, the formal cause, the final or motive cause, and lastly, the efficient cause.

The *matter* is some particular fault from which our chief difficulties arise; or virtue opposed to it, the virtue we most require. The *form* includes the resolution we made in the morning respecting the said fault or virtue; a special watchfulness throughout the day not to fall into this fault, or to perform a certain number of acts of the opposite virtue; a self-examination at noon and at night whether we have fallen into the fault or exercised the virtue; a comparison of periods of time, so that we may ascertain our gain or our loss.

The *end* is the extirpation of this fault, or the acquisition of the opposite virtue. Lastly, the *efficient cause* is any human being, zealous for his advancement in virtue, who will devote himself to this exercise.

I propose now to enter into all these points more in detail. May God grant grace to my words, that I may do justice to the value of this valuable exercise, and may induce my readers to undertake it in great earnestness, if they really desire to advance in the way of perfection.

In the first place, it must be borne in mind that this Examen is a contest against our faults. The contest is a painful one, for it is fought out in our own interior; it is a protracted one, for it ends only with life; it is fought with risks, for few escape altogether unhurt from it; the victory is uncertain, for unless God by His grace strengthen our weakness, we shall certainly be overthrown and defeated in this battle. St. Augustine says, "We are engaged in a daily fight in our heart; man contends single-handed in his heart against a host. Avarice makes its suggestions; lust makes its suggestions; gluttony its suggestions; the joys of popularity make theirs. Suggestions assail him from all sides; he refuses himself to all; he answers all; he turns away from all; he will not easily escape a wound from all his enemies."*

No one will deny that the paths of spiritual life lie in the midst of a certain sweetness and confidence, trust, hope, and even security. For what sweetness can compare with the sweetness of conversing with God? What hope so precious as that which promises the possession of the Divinity? What security equal to that of having God Himself for our friend and our ally in war? At the same time it must be acknowledged, this most delightful path is rendered difficult and rugged by the task of overcoming our faults. "One thing," says à Kempis, "withholds many from progress and fervent emendation, to wit, the dread of the difficulty and the efforts of the struggle. For those above all others make the greatest progress in virtue, who most bravely attempt to overcome the things that are most difficult and arduous to them. For a man advances more, and deserves more abundant graces in those matters in which he most overcomes himself and mortifies himself interiorly."†

This writer goes on to suggest the matter for the Particular Examen—"Two things most conduce to great correction: viz., to withdraw oneself with energy from the objects to which nature is viciously inclined, and fervently to pursue the good, which is most needed by us." And he warns us of the difficulty of the contest, "that the task of resisting our vices and

---

* *In Psalm.* xcix. 1.   † L. i., cap. xxv., nn. 3, 4.

passions is more severe than the heaviest bodily toil." So that no one may be misled, and after foolishly and presumptuously entering the arena, throw away his shield and seek safety in flight.

Perhaps this explains why many persons begin the contest of this Examen, but few persevere with it. A vast host, and more than thirty thousand, went forth under Gideon against the Madianites. But when this force came in sight of the enemy, two and twenty thousand, overcome by fear, returned to their homes. Of the ten thousand left, a great number, unable to endure their thirst, cast themselves on their knees, and putting their mouths to the stream, quenched their parched throats with copious draughts. Only three hundred contented themselves with the water they caught in their hands as they passed along. And those only who satisfied their thirst in moderation would the Lord admit to share the victory over the enemy.

May God open the eyes of those blind persons who do not see that what befell Gideon's soldiers daily happens to them. For many there are who gladly buckle on their armour to do battle with the enemies of the soul; but fly away, scared and conquered by the difficulty. When they are in the presence of the enemy, and the combat is about to commence, they are overcome by the thirst after temporal goods, they bend their knees to the ground, they turn aside to worldly concerns, they wish to quench their thirst in the waters of Egypt, though not all the cisterns of Egypt shall satisfy them. Of these craven soldiers, some who had put their hand to the plough of perfection have gone back to the world and its follies; others, indeed, remain in the Religious state which they had embraced, but have none of its spirit—they lack the courage to fight the battles of the Lord, but they choose to wear the livery of His soldiers.

Of the former class, some were led to the world by the *foot of pride;** for, vanquished by the vanity of their hearts, they shrink from ignominy, they fly ill-treatment, the lowliness of Christ they shun, and, after aiming at great and high thoughts, they fall headlong into the precipice of endless shame. Others of this class were seduced by the *concupiscence of the flesh.* After abandoning the army of God, they sit down with their wickedness before the flesh-pots of Egypt, they stain the white garment of the soul with their sins of lust, they destroy their beauty, they tarnish their glory, they—like unclean animals—wallow in their own mire. Others, enslaved to other vices, look again towards the world and turn back.

All, having consecrated themselves to the heavenly warfare, recoil from the contest; they dread the fight with themselves, with their passions, with their sins. Though false to themselves, these soldiers, having left the ranks of the brave and returned to their homes, do not inflict much injury on their comrades; they cease to shock, by their unworthy conduct, those who persevere manfully. Hence God of old commanded that when the people went forth to war, those who lacked courage should be excluded from the army, and the captains addressed every band—" *What man is there that is fearful and fainthearted?* Let him go

* Psalm xxxv. 12.

and return to his house, lest he make the hearts of his brethren to fear, as he himself is possessed with fear."*

Of the fainthearted, however, not a few who shrink from battle remain with the army; and though, with their comrades, they have taken the oath to destroy the passions which stand in their way, they still keep up a friendship with their vices and passions when they neglect the Particular Examen. These persons would fain reconcile the flesh and the spirit, vice and virtue; they wish to give something to the spirit and something to the flesh; they will not deny their passions always, they will sometimes let virtue carry the day. Such persons may be likened to Issachar, the son of Jacob, regarding whom the holy Patriarch prophesied—"*Issachar shall be a strong ass, lying down between the borders. He saw rest that it was good; and the land that it was excellent. And he bowed his shoulder to carry, and became a servant under tribute.*"†

The cudgel cannot prevent the ass from taking his mouthful, once he has found his way into the green meadow. The ass will obey his master, but when the occasion offers he will follow his own bent. Such are they who fear to attack their vices. They seek *rest*, and they prefer *rest* to fighting. They lie down between the borders, that is, between the borders of the spirit and the flesh; and, as they prize peace, they are willing to pay tribute to both, that so they may escape contending with either. The tribute they pay to the spirit consists in certain penitential deeds, certain mortifications and exterior observances; for

* Deut. xx. 8. † Gen. xlix. 14.

the most part they discharge these with a bad grace, and gain little by them. The tribute they pay to the flesh consists in anxieties concerning worldly and temporal matters, excessive attention to matters which concern not their state, unceasing restlessness, and remorse of conscience. What liberty of spirit can the soul enjoy which is burdened with such heavy tribute, and, *lying between the borders*, serves two masters? Such a one is so far a spiritual man as outwardly to obtain the reputation of being such; he is so far an interior man that without a teacher he can discourse on conscience matters. He is familiar with the word "Particular Examen," but he knows nothing of its virtue. For as this exercise is very effectual and chases away sloth, these persons can never understand the nature and efficacy of the Examen, unless they change their dispositions and reduce to subjection their disordered thoughts and desires. Persons of this description often cause much mischief in Community life to the fervent. For the soldiers of God who aspire to a truly spiritual life, and even to perfection, do not care to waste their strength in the pursuit. When, then, they watch their cowardly brethren, who in deeds and words profess to have found peace without any such severe struggles; when they hear that the perfection at which they aim is not inconsistent with a desire for honour, for self-ease, or with the flight of those things which wound self-respect or self-ease, or with the enjoyment of small gratifications, how easily the valiant soldier may lend himself to such vile models!

CHAPTER II.

FROM WHAT CAUSES THE NEGLECT OF THIS EXAMEN ARISES.

THIS neglect arises from three causes. The first is that the soul is contented with a low degree of virtue, and does not aspire to high perfection. Such a one neglects the Examen, because it does not fall in with the view which he proposes to himself, for he is not really anxious to correct his lesser faults.

The second is that the soul, though anxious for higher perfection, despairs of attaining it; he considers the rebellion of his nature, the strength of his passions, the force of his evil habits, and the hindrances arising from his occupations, and hence he loses heart, and imagines he cannot with ten thousand men resist the enemy who encounters him with twenty thousand; therefore he lays down his arms and sues for peace.

The third is that the soul, though eager for the attainment of perfection, and though free from diffidence, does not employ every means, but such only as are easy and more agreeable to his disposition. Therefore he prefers prayer and contemplation to the mortification of his passions, and he would sooner devote two or three hours to recollection and union with God, than give half an hour to the Examen. He will pretend that the liberty of the spirit is restrained by these repeated self-examinations, and he will think that it is better to be drawn sweetly to union with God than to bend his thoughts vigorously to the task of the Examen.

By what words, or by what considerations, can we more effectually rouse those who tamely acquiesce in a low degree of virtue, and induce them to turn their eyes to the higher perfection of interior life placed within their reach by the grace of God, than by those addressed by St. Jerome to the noble virgin Demetrias, encouraging her, zealous as she was, to advance to gain the summit of virtue.

"Men are never satisfied with some progress in the pursuits of the world; shall we be satisfied to have made a beginning in virtue? In earthly pursuits we are full of eagerness, and we only grow cold when there is question of Heaven. In matters of trifling moment we overflow with zeal, and are only indifferent regarding the loftiest objects. We ought to blush when we see the zeal and the care with which men seek to perfect themselves in knowledge. The thirst for literary excellence is not quenched by years; nay, I may say, with a worldly writer, it grows with advancing age. The thirst for riches is insatiable; the craving for wealth knows no limits. Objects which must perish so quickly are sought so unceasingly. And we yield to a sluggish indifference, and do not care to obtain divine knowledge, heavenly riches, immortal glory; the riches of the interior life we scarcely deign to look upon, and if we touch them ever so lightly we imagine ourselves sated. Far otherwise is the invitation given by Divine Wisdom to Its banquet. *They that eat Me shall yet hunger, and they that drink Me shall yet thirst.'** No one is ever filled at this banquet; no one is palled with satiety. The greater the desire and appetite for this food, the more shall be given. Our Lord says in the Gospel—*'Blessed are they who hunger and thirst after justice, for they shall be filled.'*† He would have us hunger and thirst after justice, that we may be filled with the reward of justice hereafter. Let us attend to the force of His words. We are to crave after justice as the starving man craves for food, or one dying from thirst craves for a draught."

These are the words of St. Jerome, and it would not be easy to adduce more urgent reasons or more striking comparisons as a reproof to tepidity—"He who shuns perfection and contents himself with mediocrity, gives a proof that his soul has never tasted the heavenly food; for as St. Gregory Nazianzen says, if you wish to attain mediocrity, you must aim at the highest."

Let us now turn to the second class. These persons desire perfection, but they have given up all hope of attaining it. For this disease we shall prescribe a remedy devised by Galen, the prince of physicians, and an illustrious teacher of Ethical Philosophy. In the first of the three books which he composed on the discovery and cure of the diseases of the soul, he recommends a method for the correction of faults very much resembling that prescribed by St. Ignatius in his Particular Examen; and he exhorts his readers to contend against their vices with all their strength, though the victories they will obtain may not be

---

* Ecclus. xxiv. 29. † St. Matt. v. 6.

thought as much of as those of Hercules, Achilles, and other noted warriors. He encourages them to hope that by persevering in the contest they may secure that perfect health which they aspire to. Galen assigns two hours for this exercise, one in the morning the other at night: in the morning the good resolution must be formed, at night the self-examination must take place. Suppose, for instance, you wish to curb your anger or any other passion. On waking, you will think of the occasions which may arise during the day, and you will reflect that a man endowed with reason should not give way to the same impulses as dumb brutes, and allow himself to be ruled by them, and you will firmly exact from yourself a resolution to avert such a disgrace. At night, before retiring to rest, renew this purpose and count up the number of times you have fallen.

But some on account of old age, others on account of faults which have become inveterate from long indulged habits, may despair of achieving a complete victory, and perhaps, as they cannot secure everything, may renounce the hope of securing anything. The wise physician writes as follows for them—"Let no one be deterred from attempting to improve himself, though even he be fifty years old and think himself marred by a vice which is not incurable or irreparable. For no one in sickness would give in to his sickness because he was fifty years old; nay, he would employ every remedy in his power to regain health, though he might be convinced he could never be as strong as Hercules." In the same way let us not be deterred from attempting to improve our souls, though we may be persuaded we shall never reach the perfection of the Wise Man. Nay, let us hope confidently we may even reach this point, if from the beginning we watch over the correction of ourselves such as we are. At least we can make sure of one point; we shall be most anxious not to be wholly deformed as was the body of Thersites. For, had we had the opportunity before our birth of meeting Him Who presided over our destiny, and had He refused our entreaty for a most robust and vigorous body, we should certainly have besought Him to grant us a body in the second, or third, or fourth degree of vigour. If we could not have the strength of Hercules, we should be pleased to have that of Achilles; and if we could not have his we should be contented with that of Ajax, or Diomede, or Agamemnon, or Patroclus; and if we could not have the strength of any of these, we should be contented with that of any illustrious hero. In the same way, I imagine, he who cannot obtain the highest excellence of mind, will aspire to be placed in the second or third, or even fourth rank. What I recommend is not a thing which is impracticable, to those at least who are willing to prove themselves and give it a serious trial for some length of time.

Galen, a Pagan teacher, merely guided by the light of reason, to our confusion instructs us and opens the paths of perfection, which so many Christians enlightened by the teaching of the Gospel refuse to see. He exhorts us to undertake a contest with our strength, which we, though armed in the power of divine grace, alas! recoil from. Not without a certain modesty he bids us, as we enter the arena, yield precedence to those who having received greater succours from the Creator of all things, and being mounted, as it were, on swifter steeds, won the goal more happily; and at least to strive to follow these men and secure the laurels of virtue to which we may aspire. He says we must make great account of this degree, though it be not the highest; and we must consider ourselves privileged, if at any cost we can attain it. Grant then, that you are not called to the perfection of a St. Ignatius, a St. Francis Xavier, or so many of our great men, but know that one of the most effectual helps by which these holy men proved themselves superior to all earthly affections was this very Particular Examen, about which I am writing; and do you make use of the same means, and follow closely, if you cannot rival, these heroes.

I must now address a word to the third class, who really aspire to perfection and are not tempted to despair of its attainment, but shrink from this battle with their passions, and betake themselves to the more quiet and genial exercises of prayer, contemplation, divine love, union with God; in fact, bury themselves in the very love of Christian perfection. But is it true that we can enter into the land flowing with milk and honey without first waging a fierce war against its inhabitants and destroying them by the sword? There are some paintings of priceless value which were executed with very little pains and labour. And there are some souls living in union with God without any internal struggle of their passions, who may be compared unto Benjamin, of whom it is written—"*The best beloved of the Lord shall dwell* *confidently in him: as in a bride-chamber shall he abide all the day long, and between his shoulders shall he rest."** A naturally happy temperament, solitude, the absence of dangerous occasions, or the special favour of God giving Himself to His creature, may have obtained for them the sweetness of internal peace, abundance of devotion, and the sensible presence of their Spouse, without being obliged to encounter their spiritual foes in deadly fight. But, generally speaking, virtues grown in the midst of such delights are frail and delicate; and they do not flourish unless supported and preserved by the same soil which gave them rise. And, therefore, virtues of this description do not befit men of our Society, "who," according to our holy Founder, "must aim at the attainment of true and solid virtues, whether they receive many or few consolations."† Now those virtues only deserve to be called solid which are acquired in war with the opposite vices, and by the acts which belong to them. These virtues do not depend on internal consolations, nor do they vanish before the fury and storms of temptations, or in the presence of dangerous occasions. These virtues are truly Apostolical virtues, such as the heralds of the Gospel ought to possess. For though the couch on which the soul reposes with her God be *flourishing*, yet "*threescore valiant ones of the most valiant of Israel surround it, all holding swords and most expert in war: every man's sword upon his thigh, because of fears in the night.*"‡ Such as these valiant ones should be the

---

* Deut. xxxiii. 12.   † *Summ.*, reg. 22.
‡ Cant. iii. 7, 8.

warriors whom God has stationed in the Church to guard those souls who are invited to the repose of contemplation. They should be equipped with virtues acquired in manly conflict, waged while some of the souls intrusted to their guidance rest peaceably in God; by their own experience must they be trained to forestall the wiles of the enemy, to withstand his onset, and to keep faithful watch and ward, lest the spouses of Christ be disturbed in this their repose and godly quiet. Now, if the care of such souls as are in close union with God demand that the ghostly Father and Master be trained by experience in the conflict with vice, how much more will he not need it, to be enabled rapidly to pass from place to place, to scour divers provinces for the direction of others, to deal with affairs of every description, to dwell amid serpents and dragons, among so many occasions, not of distractions and of inward dryness only, but of grievous falls. This is the reason which urged our holy Father Ignatius to special accuracy and minuteness in his treatise on this practice, seeing it was most befitting and proper to his sons. Nor did he act thus with a view to our inculcating it on others whose spiritual welfare concerns us, but in order that we, whose chief and main end is *to devote ourselves to the salvation and perfection of our own souls*, should become familiar with the use thereof. If we but duly consider this end, and at the same time advert to those uprisings of nature we are ever and anon liable to, the source of which is in the violence of our passions, or the force of habits contracted in the world, or in the distractions arising from multifarious occupations and engagements, and in the numberless temptations that spring therefrom, or else, in the defect of devotion, in dryness at prayer, we shall be convinced that for each and all of these reasons, they who have constant dealings with men, and are bound to show them the way of salvation, both by word and example, must, unless they wish to run themselves into danger, be endowed with solid, well grounded—I had almost said adamantine—virtues, which have been invigorated by a lengthened conflict; that the model of such should be the returned captives of Israel, "*who with the one hand did their work, and with the other grasped a sword*,"* since it is incumbent upon them to wage war on the vices of others and on their own passions.

To sum up this chapter, we may then say, that the Particular Examen is a kind of war against vices which must never be suspended, whether from faintheartedness or fear of difficulties, or from our resting content with a certain mediocrity of virtue, or from despair of attaining perfection, or through our taking up other practices more congenial to our tastes. It remains for us to unfold the original plan traced by St. Ignatius; to wit, the form thereof, and the matter (which is the vice to be uprooted, or its opposite virtue), the times and other circumstances.

* 2 Esdras iv. 17.

CHAPTER III.

THE FORM OR METHOD OF THIS EXAMEN, BEGINNING WITH THE RESOLVE TO BE MADE ON RISING.

THE form or method of the Particular Examen may be brought under four points. First, every morning at rising we must make a firm purpose concerning the vice we are combatting, or the virtue we are striving after. Second, we must take care during the course of the day to carry out this purpose. Third, we must call ourselves to account for the shortcomings into which we may have fallen. Fourth, we must compare days and weeks together, so as to take the measure of either our progress or decline. The first point of this exercise—the first step therein, so to speak, is the morning resolution, concerning which our holy Father writes as follows—"*The first time is in the morning when, as soon as we rise, we should resolve to keep strict guard over ourselves in the matter of the sin or evil habit we wish to correct.*"

Hereon, we may observe, first, that by a resolution or purpose is meant a steady determination of the will concerning something difficult, a purpose liable to contradiction or opposition in its fulfilment. For in easy things, a simple motion of the will is enough, its consent is all that is needed for the completion of the work. But in what is more difficult, to will alone does not suffice, but the constraining power of the will needs bracing up, and it is this which properly is called a purpose or resolution. The Apostle in

treating of virginity makes this distinction between simple volition and purpose; for he speaks in different terms of a father who gives his daughters in marriage, and of one who endeavours to keep them from the nuptial couch. Of the former, as what they have to do is easy and conformable to natural inclination, he says—"*If any man thinks that he is behaving himself unseemly towards his virgin daughter in case she should pass the flower of her age, and if it must needs be so, let him do what he will, he sinneth not if she marry.*" *
But of the latter class, as their task is in no wise easy, he says—"*He that standeth steadfast in his heart, having no necessity, and hath power in respect of his will, and hath determined this in his own heart, that he will keep his virgin daughter, shall do well.*" †

Thus may it be seen that he terms an arduous resolve, demanding serious deliberation and steadfast performance, a determination, which is just what St. Ignatius calls a resolution. To this may we deem that the Psalmist alludes when taking into consideration the frailty of our nature, the revolt and resistance of the appetite, he speaks as follows of the observance of God's commandments—"*I have sworn and have steadfastly purposed to keep Thy righteous commandments.*" ‡

As you see, not only did he steadfastly purpose, but he swore. Whence it may be inferred that the Psalmist came to that resolution after he had been made aware of the difficulties in the fulfilment of these righteous judgments. These same difficulties meet us in the Particular Examen. We declare war

* 1 Cor. vii. 36.   † 1 Cor. vii. 37.
‡ Psalm cxviii. 106.

The Form or Method of this Examen. 21

against that vice which troubles us most. The first step to be taken in this war is to send a challenge to the foe, in other words, to make a resolution against it.

Second, it is to be observed that such a resolution is the end of prayer, of our meditation, of the general examen, while it forms the starting-point of the Particular Examen, as was noticed heretofore. For in the method of our holy Founder, the end and aim of prayer is to stir up the will, as is plain throughout the first Exercise of the "Three Powers." That the end of these motions and affections is to be good resolves, is evident from the colloquy of the Exercise, where it is said—"*I will further call myself to account, asking what I have hitherto done for Christ worthy of remembrance, what I am willing, or what I ought to do.*" What means this last clause—"*What am I willing, or what ought I to do?*" Naught else but the resolution we should make. The same appears no less unmistakeably from numerous other passages, which show that the sole aim of the Exercises is to elicit the resolve to reform our conduct, for God's greater glory. This too is the end of the general examen, the fifth and last point of which is concerned with the purpose of amendment. The reason of all this is obvious, seeing that the end of all these Exercises of St. Ignatius is none other but a godly life and the sanctification of our soul. Now the main source of a godly life and of sanctification, is practically a good purpose. Hence the aim and outcome of these Exercises can be naught else but this resolve. Fitly then does the author of Ecclesiasticus warn us to set great store by a good resolution—"*Let the good counsel of thine own heart be steadfast.*" Bind thyself by a steadfast purpose of performing that which thou hast rightly devised. "*For nothing is more precious to thee than it.*"* In other words, nothing can be of greater advantage. He at once proceeds to prove this point, showing that such a purpose secures and directs all our doings—"*Let truth go before thy every action, and a steadfast counsel before every deed.*"† In other words, delude not thyself, but in all thine actions carry out thy resolutions. Now as it is to this performance of what has been resolved upon in the Exercises that the Particular Examen is directed, it starts with the resolution which is the goal of all the other Exercises. Thus may we perceive the connection and interdependence of the several Exercises. Meditation and the general examen tend to the formation of a good resolution; the Particular Examen ensures its fulfilment. Herein, too, may we appreciate the dexterity and profound insight wherewith St. Ignatius leads on souls to perfection.

At the very beginning of his work, he prescribes a scrutiny of our sins and usual defects by the general examen, in order that we may attain the knowledge of our actual state and progress, and discover by what passions we are more violently urged on, what are the inclinations which more vehemently bear us along, what evil habits we are most prone to, to what vices we most frequently yield. He next presents meditation as a means of self-improvement, and of making resolutions to uproot our vices, and of

* Ecclus. xxxvii. 17.   † Ecclus. xxxvii. 20.

implanting in their stead the opposite virtues. And that each resolution may be effectually reduced to practice, he will have us to wage war on each vice singly.

He maps out the plan of this war, which is to make a particular resolution against the predominant vice; when we fall, to take courage; as is the wont with wrestlers, to renew our purpose until we have utterly worsted the foe. What more easy, or sweeter, could be devised as a stay to our weakness, than to warn us not to lose heart, even though we be damaged in the conflict? What more fitted to stir up our fervour than to arise after a fall, and to renew the struggle with no less ardour than if we had never been worsted? What method could be devised more conformable to our nature and to man's want, than to meditate in order to come to a resolve, to resolve in order to a practical fulfilment, to fulfil one's purpose with a view to habituating one's self to well-doing, to destroy by such habit the evil opposed to it? Thus it is obvious that this practice of making a purpose is of immense efficacy, while its mildness is no less so; that it supports our frailty and maintains us in our struggle against vice in a happy medium between two extremes, which being extremes, cannot but make us deviate from the path of virtue.

These two extremes are indiscreet fervour and languor, both of which tend to make us weary of that constant renewal of our purpose required by this exercise. As regards indiscreet fervour, some folks are transported by so vehement an emotion, as to deem it enough for them to make but one resolve against a vice, or passion, in order to be wholly rid of any further disturbance; they will never feel the temptation to anger, after having once for all resolved to practise meekness, and not to yield to passion; they will never break forth into murmuring and grumbling, when they have once determined to renounce the vice. What, then, is the consequence? When they relapse into these faults, they grieve, and torment themselves at being made aware of their weakness, and at discovering that what they fancied they had accomplished still remains to be done. Thus do they betray their utter ignorance of the way to extirpate vice and to implant virtue. They think that it is to be done at one stroke, even as a statue of molten brass takes shape the instant it is cast into the mould. They want their ailments to be cured forthwith, and, as it were, by a miracle, in a single instant. Bleeding and cathartics they despise; they wish to pass without an interval from sickness to perfect health, without undergoing any curative treatment. They seek to fly without wings, to scale a tower without ladders, to clear at one bound the course of all the virtues. Therefore are they ever sticking to the starting-post, at the same distance from the goal. An error held by some in days of yore was, that the victory over our passions could reach to a kind of apathy, or insensibility, whereby the soul is so steadfastly grounded in virtue that on no occasion whatever could the mind deflect, be it never so little, from the straight path of right, but rather would it with unruffled calm, and without struggle, be wholly addicted to virtue. But this was a day-dream of men brought to vanity in their reasonings, confounding the time of conflict with that of rest and recompense, and attributing to this period of warfare what belongs to the life of bliss. Though this figment has long since been exploded, we still meet with many who order their lives as if they were passionless. They make no effort to extirpate their evil habits, or to contract good ones by the appropriate acts; but flatter themselves that they have demolished their passions, as was the fate of the Philistine giant, at a single stroke.

This fond fancy is not only profitless; it is, moreover, harmful in several ways. First, the violence these people do themselves is ofttimes prejudicial to bodily health. Now, want of health, especially with beginners, not uncommonly proves a formidable obstacle to perfection, in that it fills the soul with fear and grief, and at the very time that the body needs severe and rigorous treatment, we have to show greater indulgence to that domestic foe, on account of its ailment. Further, it is a usual artifice of the devil to inspire an exaggerated fervour, in order that excessive rigour may degenerate into laxity. "You yourselves have had experience," says St. Bernard to his brethren, "how some (to your confusion be it said), who at the outset could not be kept back (such was the vehemence and ardour with which they were impelled onwards), have at length sunk to such a depth of sloth that, to use the words of the Apostle, 'After having begun with the spirit, they are now absorbed in the flesh.'"*

* *Serm.* xxxiii. *on the Canticles.*

An indiscreet fervour in subjugating our passions is wont to bring on bodily ailments, which in their turn engender self-indulgence and softness. Besides which, the virtues which owe their origin to this headlong violence, are not of the temper to be relied upon in occasions of trial. For as a stone upheld by sheer force in the air, when let go, falls with no less impetus than had it not been upheld, so the passions which are not subdued by opposite habits, but are violently checked, will be found to be no less lively and vigorous than at the beginning. For as nought that is violent can endure, it must needs be that this violence will come to an end. Wherefore, when the soul, tired out, slackens in its effort, it finds itself after all as imperfect as if it had never made a beginning. The devil has at this point another weapon in reserve—the temptation, that is, to grievous despair. For even as a wayfarer who strives to reach to the summit of a lofty mountain, but, having thoughtlessly chosen the path which to him seemed the shortest and most direct, loses heart at finding his strength overtaxed by the obstacles he meets with, and thinking there is no other road, gives up the ascent in despair and returns to the level plain; so, too, do they who have set themselves the task of ridding themselves forthwith of their passions, and of practising in all perfection the virtues they have determined upon but a moment since, when coming to the reality they discover that it is more than a match for them, lay down their arms, deem perfection an impossibility, and return to the common beaten track. This temptation is not unlike what St. Ignatius mentions in his Fourth Rule on Scruples—"*The enemy is wont to watch craftily what manner of conscience each soul has, whether it be rough-grained or delicate. If the latter, he strives to render it more delicate, and to bring it to an extreme degree of anxiety, in order that when he has cruelly disturbed it he may deter it from all spiritual progress.* For instance, if he finds a soul that yields to no sin, whether mortal or venial, that shrinks (so to speak) from the very shadow of any wilful transgression; as he cannot *reproach it with any real sin, he endeavours to make it perceive sin where there is none, as, for example, in some word or passing thought.*" What is his aim? It is to render the conscience so delicate, as wholly to destroy it. For the soul, finding it cannot avoid what it falsely deems to be sin, falls without misgiving into real sins. The enemy follows an opposite method with such as are gifted with a looser conscience, as St. Ignatius proceeds to show in the same rule. "He strives, on the other hand, to render a lax conscience still more lax, to the end that, having heretofore made light of venial faults, it may daily grow more careless and *unconcerned about mortal sins.*"

Such, then, is the artifice of the enemy. He strives to push every one to the side to which he finds him to have a leaning, in order to land him in an extreme. He makes use of this stratagem in the very matter of good purpose wherewith we are dealing. For if he come in contact with an ardent soul eager to subject its passions to reason, to uproot its evil habits, he spurs it on while running full tilt, and urges it to attempt to complete its undertaking within the brief space of an hour. If, on the contrary, the soul be torpid and diffident, he intensifies this torpor, and endeavours to bring to pass that it should not make one good resolve throughout the year. We must, then, hold fast to what St. Ignatius lays down in the following Rule — "In order to advance in the spiritual path, the soul must ever tend to the opposite of that to which the enemy strives to drag it. So that if he endeavour to make the conscience still more lax, we should make it more strict, and relax it when he tries to bind it too tightly. Thus, by keeping aloof from the dangers of either extreme, will the soul abide in tranquil medium and in a state of safety." We may here, in passing, call attention to St. Ignatius' extraordinary prudence, which shines forth in this rule. For to the slothfully inclined we must uncompromisingly prescribe that they follow after fervour, and make their conscience more strict. We must, indeed, guard against the extreme of an excessive fervour; but the danger of such as these falling into it is very remote. No so with those who lean to an excessive strictness. Not that we are to advise them needlessly to follow a lax and tepid conscience (this were too dangerous a counsel for our corrupt nature); they are to be told to avoid the extreme, and to establish themselves calmly and securely in a medium state. The Latin version quoted above, in prescribing for such a certain relaxation or laxity, clearly means that they are to be kept from either extreme, not that they are to be driven into an opposite one. This is plain from the wording of the Spanish original, which is literally as follows—"*If the enemy strive to make the conscience too lax, he should make it more strict; if the enemy strive to make it too strict, so as to draw it to an extreme, the soul is to try to establish itself in the middle, so that it may be wholly at peace.*" But what is this middle state? It is fervently to resolve against, and manfully to resist, the vice we are contending with.

We presuppose all along that this conflict is to be an enduring one, since death alone can bring undisturbed peace. Nor in so protracted a struggle can we fail to receive wounds which must be healed by penance. And the contest will have to be renewed by fresh purposes against the enemy that has laid us low. Such is the way to subdue our vicious habits, to get rid of our perverse inclinations; not indeed by smothering them at one effort, that were impossible, but by gradually weakening them, bearing patiently with their uprising, and beating back their assaults with earnestness.

In the other extreme are to be found those who never have any fixed or settled purpose, but whose spiritual progress is wholly limited to certain inward devotions and consolations, and some outward austerities or penalties; for the rest, they give themselves up to the guidance of their inclinations, and are carried away by the torrent of their evil habits. Souls such as these may never hope to attain real or solid virtues and true detachment of heart, which in our miserable fallen state cannot be acquired without violence and conflict. Now, where this cannot be shirked, there must needs be a resolution, which, as we have observed, requires a resolve. Now a resolve, as we said heretofore, is but a bracing up of the will to a struggle with some difficulty repugnant to our natural inclination. Since, then, to lay down one's arms is to avow a defeat, the same may be said of one who desists from making a resolve; for, like one who is worsted, he gives his ghostly foe an opportunity of putting forth all his strength, and of winning a victory. For he that makes a resolve withstands his vices, for it is by this the struggle begins. He, then, that does not make any resolution (who may be called a purposeless man), as well as he who persists not in his resolve, yields without a struggle to his antagonists. Rightly is it asserted by the author of the *Imitation of Christ*, that "the origin of every evil temptation is instability of soul."* He calls an evil temptation that which overcomes the soul and obtains its purpose. A temptation which does not succeed, but which the will rejects, is not evil, but advantageous to him who gains a victory over his enemy. The origin of our disasters and of the victory of the tempter is *instability* of soul, or not keeping to our resolve. The same author sets this forth in a very apt similitude—"For," says he, "as a ship without a rudder is tossed to and fro by the waves, so is a slothful man who keeps not to his resolution tempted in manifold ways." No comparison could more aptly fit the case of a soul assailed by temptations, which are like the waves of a raging sea. "*They mount up to heaven, and go down even to the depths.*"† The security against shipwreck is in the rudder, for as St. James says—"*Behold ships, althought they be so great, and are driven by fierce winds,*

---

* Book i., chap. xiii., n. 5. † Psalm cvi. 26.

yet are they turned about with a very small rudder whithersoever the desire of the helmsman willeth." It is with this that the pilot steers the ship, ploughs the waves, makes a stand against the winds, and surmounts the raging billows. Now, what a ship's rudder is in a storm, gives us to understand what a firm purpose does for one under temptation. For if he will but stand to it, he steadies himself, governs his actions, and defends himself from the waves of temptation which beat against his resolution. Should the ship lose its rudder, shipwreck is inevitable. So does a soul without resolution yield to temptation. All that we have set forth in this chapter may be made clear by this one comparison, which, at the same time, sets forth the way wherein we are to wage war on our vices. We must make resolutions, and that constantly, nor deem the battle over after we have formed our purpose, as if our passions were forthwith brought under, and our evil habits overcome. For like as neither the rudder, nor the cunning of the pilot, nor the labours of the crew ever on the alert, can avail to hinder the vessel from being continually tossed and from shipping seas; like as a ship cannot be still amid a raging sea; as a captain cannot reasonably expect that his passengers will, in rough weather, go through their voyage without sea-sickness; as it is ever necessary for the pilot to keep his eyes fixed on the compass, and his hand to the helm, especially when the winds are high, if he really intend to reach the port he has set out for—the same holds good of our spiritual navigation. For though a firm resolve be in the truest

* St. James iii. 4.

sense the rudder of our soul, by means of which, under the inspirations of divine grace, we are to make the harbour of virtue, yet does it not calm the tumult of our passions, nor, owing to our frailty and heedlessness, hinder our craft from leaking at several points, so that we must needs renew our purpose, and lighten our vessel by means of repentance.

We may find another no less apt illustration in the great tidal rivers; unless their waters be kept confined within their banks, they will overflow and destroy crops, the hopes of a future harvest, cattle, flocks, forests, men, and whole cities, and will overwhelm whatever they meet in their course. Our passions, unless checked, do us no less harm. Now, that which opposes their violence, is our resolution to go counter to them. This it is which, like a bank or earthwork, deadens and holds their violence in check. And even as the rivers already mentioned are not deprived of their destructive force by the precautions taken against it, but are ever in conflict with those who, by raising banks or by other contrivances, impede their overflow and confine them within their bed; as, too, we must never cease from strengthening the obstacles we put in their way until the might of their tempestuous waves are broken, and they be securely kept within limits—thus are we to control our passions, as they are far more pertinacious, nor to be subdued by one resolution, but by repeated purposes persevered in until our will is ready to forego what is forbidden, and to rest content within the boundaries of what is virtuous and lawful.

It is thus obvious that our war against our vices

must begin with a resolution, and likewise that such resolution does not deprive our evil habits of their strength, nor prevent them from warring against us, and from striving to overthrow our resolution. In this twofold conflict we must, therefore, take it for granted that our resolve will not render us invulnerable, and that we should not lose heart when stricken by the foe. This is, in substance, the advice of the author of the *Imitation of Christ*, who on the first point observes—" Let us strive as much as we like, yet shall we fail slightly in many things."* On the second, he says—" If he that makes a firm purpose falls short, what will that man do who seldom or feebly purposes?"†

* Book i., chap. xix., n. 3.   † Book i., chap. xix., n. 2.

CHAPTER IV.

ON THE QUALITIES REQUISITE FOR A GOOD PURPOSE.

To bear fruit, it is requisite that a resolution have (1) a determinate matter; it demands (2) discretion in order to be effectual; (3) steadfastness, lest it be easily set aside; (4) humility, so as not to lean on its own strength; (5) daily increase that it may attain the summit of perfection.

To begin, then, we must not rest satisfied with vague and general resolves, as were that of keeping God's commandments, or of striving after the perfection proper to our state, but as the author of the *Imitation of Christ* aptly warns us—"We must ever purpose something definite."* It must be such as to be distinctly realized by the understanding. We are next to make a return on ourselves to inquire whether we really do fulfil what we purpose, and add thereto an examen as to whether we have fulfilled it. For as men's actions are concerned with determinate and individual objects, indefinite purposes can have no fulfilment, unless they be restricted to something in particular. Hence the Apostle saith—"*I therefore so run, as not uncertainly; so fight I, as not beating the air.*"†
For of a truth, he is beating the air and runs aimlessly, whose purposes are indefinite and general.

Next, the resolution must be discreet—proportioned, that is, to our actual powers of body and mind. "*Seek*

---

* Book i., chap. ix., n. 3.
† 1 Cor. ix. 26.

not what is above thee," * is the warning of the Holy Ghost. For even as a traveller to a far off country, first sets before him the land he intends to reach, and then maps out a direct and well defined road to be kept to from the outset to the term of his journey, and having once started makes use of prudence and caution lest he exhaust himself by overhaste, or linger on the road by being too slow; and then divides his journey into daily stages of so many miles or leagues; the like holds good of the matter now under treatment. Here too, after determining in particular what are the actions we undertake to amend, those especially with which we have to make a beginning, we must next have recourse to discretion, and forecaste the accidents and difficulties of the path on which we are about to enter, and take in hand forthwith some less difficulty which is within reach, nor out of proportion with our present disposition. More of this anon, when we shall have come to the object of this kind of examen, and shall explain why the conflict with a single vice, and the striving after one virtue requires to be thus minutely divided into parts. For though all our hopes must rest on the aid and almighty power of God, which is well able mightily and swiftly to overcome all difficulties, yet is it the wont of His Providence to order all things sweetly. To these two qualities must be added a third, to wit—our purpose should be steadfast, and not liable to waver. This steadfastness regards both the time when we resolve, and the moment of execution. Some resolutions are so faint at the very outset, that it is obvious they

---

* Ecclus. iii. 22.

cannot be lasting, but are wanting in strength to cope with temptation. Let each one observe in what wise men usually resolve to increase their gains, and to avoid future loss, and determine to shape on their model our strivings to diminish our vices and to grow in virtue. This is the aim of the admonition of the Wise Man—"*If thou call upon wisdom and bow down thy heart to knowledge, if thou seek her like money, and dig for her as for treasures, then shalt thou understand the fear of the Lord, and shalt find the knowledge of God.*"* Money is sought after with anxiety, and treasures are dug up from the bowels of the earth with toil; these are in a measure needed for the acquisition of spiritual store. Feeble resolves are like the purposes of sleepy people, or of the same kind as those formed by the sluggard, who, disputing with his pillow, does nought but softly turn on the other side. To such as he doth the Holy Ghost say—"*How long wilt thou sleep, thou sluggard? When wilt thou arise from thy slumbers? A little more sleep, yet a little slumber, a little folding of the hands to sleep.*"† Like as the will of the sluggard is not what it seems to be, so neither do such resolutions find their fulfilment in action, for after manifold and magnificent purposes the man grows old in a deplorable plight. Let then your resolves be steadfast and high-minded, lively, and conceived in great fervour when you make them.

But this steadfastness is no less needed when the time comes for action. A falling short on this head may have a twofold origin, either in the feebleness of judgment, or in the faint-heartedness of the will. By

---

* Prov. ii. 3, 4, 5. † Prov. vi. 9, 10.

the former, I mean that which causes us to withdraw from what we have proposed, though no fresh motives, or sufficient ones, occur to us. I have dealt with this more fully in part i., book ii., chapter xxxi., of the *Spiritual Path*.

St. Ignatius holds up this failing to reproof where he says—"*If any one hath chosen aught that can be changed, with due method and order, apart from all bias of the world, and of the flesh* (apart, that is, from all carnal or worldly motive), *he has no reason for reversing his choice, but should rather strive to advance more and more therein.*"* This failing arises, likewise, from the faint-heartedness of our will in the case, when the resolution still endures, but is broken at the time of execution, and when the soul shrinks within itself on beholding the difficulty. Of these has Solomon meetly written, "*The sluggard desires, and desires not.*"† He desires when making his resolution, he withdraws from his desire when he becomes aware of the difficulty attending it. He desires while as yet he has nothing to do, but he desires not when the work has to be taken in hand. He desires when pondering the beauty of virtue and its rewards, but desires not when he finds that this flower is hedged round by thorns. Thus does it come to pass, as Solomon bears witness, that his desires and purposes vanish in thin air, "*Like clouds and winds without rain is whoso boasteth himself and keeps not his promises.*"‡

---

* "Introduction to the knowledge of the objects of election," point iv.

† Prov. xiii. 4.

‡ Prov. xxv. 14.

"Meetly," says Venerable Bede, "is he called a sluggard, who would reign with Christ, and will not strive with Christ, who takes delight in the reward, but flinches from the conflict when commanded. Concerning such does St. James say, "*He is a double-minded man, unstable in all his ways.*"* And Ecclesiasticus—"*Woe be to double hearts . . . and to the sinner that goeth two ways.*"† For such a one goes two ways, that of perfection he resolves upon, and the way of his lusts, wherein he really walks. He goes by the former in design and purpose, but in the latter by deed and performance. It is as if two souls dwelt within a man of this sort; and, in truth, he has a twofold tendency; the one inclining him to what is perfect, the other to imperfection and evil. While endeavouring to follow both, he halts in either path.

There is but one remedy for him who suffers under this ailment; it is to consider attentively the term and end of his ways, and not to be deterred by difficulties, for "*Narrow is the way that leadeth unto life.*"‡ Of the other way, it is written, "*There is a way that seemeth right unto a man, but the end thereof are the ways of death.*"§ The rigour of God's judgments may spur the slothful man into action, as the Psalmist bears record of himself—"*I remembered Thy judgments of old, O Lord, and comforted myself.*"‖ St. Ambrose observes hereon—"Unless each one be grounded, and trained by the examples under the law, and believe the judgments of God to be sure, he will soon turn aside from the law." The judgments God,

---

* St. James i. 8.   † Ecclus. ii. 14.
‡ Matt. vii. 14.   § Prov. xvi. 25.   ‖ Psalm cxviii. 52.

as executed from the beginning of the world, are hidden from none, those that remain to be executed at the end will be made manifest. "By this remembrance," says the Psalmist, "*have I comforted myself*," which means, in St. Augustine's view of this passage— I have been roused and stirred up. For this remembrance is a powerful inducement to break through difficulties, be they what they may. To conclude, then, we must steadfastly resolve, and courageously perform, after the example of him who exclaims—"*I have sworn and have steadfastly proposed to keep Thy just judgments*"* Showing by his oath the steadfastness of his resolve, as St. Augustine explains it— "For he calls that an oath which he had steadfastly proposed by a holy vow. For the soul should be as firm in the observance of God's righteous commandments, as it ought ever to be in keeping to the oath whereby it has pledged itself."

* Psalm cxviii. 106.

CHAPTER V.

OF TWO OTHER QUALITIES OF A GOOD RESOLUTION.

THE fourth requisite is that the resolution be humble, which contributes in no small degree to its stability. For like as the solidity of a building rests on the foundations thereof, so does the stability of our purposes rest on humility, which is the groundwork of every virtue. We frequently fall short of our resolves through timidity and distrust, both of which obstacles arise from our comparing the difficulties we have to overcome with our own strength, not with that of God and of His gracious aid. If God's help be at hand, what can we resolve upon that we shall be unable to perform. As the author of the *Imitation of Christ* says—"The resolutions of the just are grounded rather upon God's grace than on their own wisdom. In it do they constantly put their trust, happen what may. For man proposes, but God disposes; nor is a man's way in his own power."* It is a mark of a humble resolution if help be sought in prayer, meditation, pious reading, the invocation of the Saints, in penances, and temporal trials, and such like, for, being the tokens of humility of heart, they greatly avail to obtain God's help. For God it is "*Who resists the proud, but gives grace to the humble.*"† On the other hand, they that rely on their own strength come to experience what the Psalmist says of himself—"*As for me, I had said in my prosperity,*

---

* Book i., chap. xix., n. 2.   † St. James iv. 6.

I shall not be moved for ever. . . . Thou didst hide Thy face from me, and I became troubled."*

A humble resolution is not on that account pusillanimous; rather does it embrace whatever it intends with God's help to overcome. Although the soul is well aware, and with the Apostle exclaims, "*I know that there dwells not in me, that is, in my flesh, any good*,"† yet is it convinced that He Who has given it to will, will also grant it to do. Wherefore, with the same Apostle does it say — "*Forgetting the things which are behind, and stretching forth unto the things that are before, I press toward the mark for the prize of the heavenly calling of God in Christ Jesus.*"‡ It should, therefore, be a settled principle with such as are desirous of making progress, that they are to put on the armour of humility, and daily to stir themselves up to an increase of perfection, which is the last quality of a good and steadfast resolution, and most necessary for all that follow after perfection. For as we read in the *Imitation of Christ*, "*The measure of our progress is in direct proportion to our resolution.*"§

We may perceive a great and manifold diversity in this regard among those that strive after virtue. Some there are who, with heroic fortitude, aspire to what is most perfect, and the greater their progress the more does their path seem to stretch out before them. Others aim, as St. Ignatius puts it, but at "*attaining a certain degree, wherein their soul may find rest.*"‖ This is but to lead the common ordinary life, free

---

* Psalm xxix. 7, 8.   † Rom. vii. 18.   ‡ Phil. iii. 13, 14.
§ Book i., chap. xix., n. 2.   ‖ *Annot.*, 18.

from all reproaches of conscience, and hence with hopes of salvation. Another set aspire not even to this, being conscious to themselves of hidden failings, and resting content with the name and repute of goodness and honesty, which causes them carefully to avoid whatever might lower them in the esteem of their fellows.

Each of these classes presents in its turn divers subdivisions and shades of difference; still, for every one does the maxim we have just now quoted hold good, "*The measure of our progress is in direct proportion to our resolution.*" Whoso aims high makes rapid progress in grace, while he that rests content with his poverty remains poor. From the beginning of one's conversion to the term thereof, our advancement is wholly made up of resolutions, more or less perfect. He, then, that is desirous of advancing must endeavour to push forward his resolutions, in order that they may tend to a yet more excellent way.

To state briefly what we have hitherto said on the formation of resolutions, I beg and pray them who have recently entered on the path of righteousness to gird themselves to keep the commandments and precepts of the Lord, with the resolve of a manful and steadfast soul, that (without any vow or oath) they may, with the Psalmist, be able to say—"*I have sworn, and have steadfastly purposed, to keep Thy righteous judgments.*" Let beginners, and such as are taken up with ridding themselves of their faults, determine to chastise their bodies, to subdue their rebellious passions, so that reason may govern appetite, that the day may dawn and the day-star which is clouded and often extinguished by the pleasures of the flesh and the allurements of sense, may arise in their hearts. Look at Daniel—"*He purposed in his heart that he would not defile himself with the portion of the King's meat, nor with the wine he drank.*"* For though the King had appointed them a daily provision of the King's meat, and of the wine he drank, he so prevailed with the prince of the eunuchs that, as he had purposed in his heart, he took no other food than water and pulse. Thus, too, Solomon, when he strove to acquire virtue—"*I thought (i.e.,* I resolved) *in my heart to withdraw myself from wine, that I might acquaint my soul with wisdom, and might avoid folly, till I might see what was good for the sons of men.*"†

They that have made progress should resolve to comply with the light from on high, and with the divine inspirations, so as to "*discern what is the will of God, good, and well-pleasing, and perfect,*"‡ and to order their doings by that light, according to that of Wisdom—"*I loved her above health and beauty, and chose to have her rather than light, for her brightness never wanes.*"§ The perfect, in other words, such as are wholly detached from all things created, and lifted up above them in order to be united with God, and to enjoy Him alone, should say, with the Psalmist—"*Whom have I in Heaven but Thee? And beside Thee there is none on earth in whom I delight.*"|| For a soul detached from things created, by prayer and contemplation is united to its Maker; wherefore the

* Dan. i. 8.   † Eccles. ii. 3.
‡ Rom. xii. 2.   § Wisdom vii. 10. || Psalm lxxii. 25.

Psalmist forthwith adds—"*As for me, to cling to God is good for me, to put my trust in the Lord my God,*" that is, in the one and only God. But as pure love is proved by works, from this love do flow works not private merely, but public, and the soul that is stable in its purposes, and laden with the fruits thereof, finds itself urged to declare before all the people the wondrous doings of God. For the Psalmist, having said that he clings to God, and that his trust is placed in Him alone, continues—" *That I may tell of all Thy works*, that is, Thy perfections, *in the gates of the daughter of Zion.*"

Such are, in a few words, the steps by which we are to advance in our resolves. Each purpose must be accompanied by works corresponding to its appropriate degree, until we have reached the summit of perfection. This will suffice for the first part of the Particular Examen, the morning resolution, to wit. Now pass we to the second part, that is, to the care wherewith we are to reduce this resolution to practice.

CHAPTER VI.

OF THE CARE WE ARE TO TAKE TO PUT OUR MORNING RESOLUTION INTO PRACTICE.

THE next part, or the second point of the Particular Examen, now comes under consideration, and it is, at the same time, its main end, to wit—that the purposes we form in the morning concerning the uprooting of vice, and the implanting of virtue, and which, for the sake of greater efficacy, we restrict to some one vice, or virtue, in particular, be put into practice. It were useless to propose what is never performed; and his labour is fruitless who strives to please God only with his will; he deludes himself who, making little of the fruit of good works, rests satisfied with the flowers of good desire. He who planted a fig-tree in his vineyard, came not to seek flowers, but fruit, and as for three years he had found no fruit, he ordered it to be cut down, saying, "*Wherefore cumbereth it the ground?*" Not that we are to infer that no account must be made of the flowers of good works; rather should we earnestly strive after them, and set great store by them, not only because of the intrinsic beauty wherewith they delight us, or the savoury smell which refreshes (such being the fruits of good purposes, by the very fact of their being formed); but mainly, because of the promise of the delicious fruits accruing from the works to be done, which are contained in these purposes as in their germ. The trees, in early spring, put forth buds, and are covered with blossoms, many of which, owing to the violence of winds, rains, and frosts, disappoint the hope of the planter. Thus, too, does our soul clothe itself with verdure, put forth blossoms in plenty, and under the genial breezes of divine grace, teem with good desires; of which few only attain the maturity of actual performance. Let the flowers of good purpose bloom luxuriantly, lest there be a dearth of the good works which are to spring therefrom. But whoso at early morn carefully gathers the dew of the divine inspiration, and abounds in good purposes, must proceed cautiously as the day speeds on, and endeavour to make the good purposes formed in the morning fructify. This care is the most important part of the Particular Examen, without which it might be said of us—"*In the morning it flourisheth and springs afresh; in the evening it is cut down and withereth.*"* This failure of our morning resolutions, and their so frequently coming to naught at their very outset, may be ascribed to two causes. To their object, on account of the greater or less difficulty we meet with in their performance; and this obstacle is met by our fervour. Or it may be attributed to the person who makes the resolution, who, through heedlessness, becomes unmindful of his purpose, so that, unwittingly, and by the force of habit and of natural inclination, he is led away from his resolve; and this is to be remedied by our carefulness. The Apostle sets forth this twofold caution in the words—"*In diligence not slothful; in spirit fervent.*"† It is a part of such diligence not to

---

* Psalm lxxxix. 6.   † Rom. xii. 11.

forget our resolution of the morning; and by fervour of spirit we are enabled to perform it. Diligence makes us beware of the occasions of the sin we propose to correct, fervour helps us to maintain our innocency when an unavoidable occasion presents itself. Diligence will make us familiarly acquainted with such considerations as help us to the virtue we aim at; fervour will, by means of them, invigorate the will. For as boiling water rises, despite the force of gravitation, and drives away the flies that approach it, so too is the soul enabled, by its fervent desires, to counteract the dead weight of its carnal propensities, and to set aside, without difficulty, harmful suggestions. But to attain this much, it is requisite that this inward fire be not newly kindled, but that it habitually burn; and diligence will feed it with meet considerations, as with fuel, and by means of meditation, as with a bellows, will direct into such a blast as to enlighten the mind thereby, and inflame the will to earnest performance. Carelessness and lukewarmness being thus got rid of, the soul becomes diligent and fervent; for without these qualities, this Examen will hardly avail it aught. Yet, if we look more closely into the subject, this twofold means may be reduced to one, to wit, to our resolution in the morning; not, indeed, a resolution either languid or wavering, but a lively, effectual, and fervent purpose, proceeding from a genuine desire to overcome the vice we are attacking, and of acquiring the opposite virtue, accompanied with an insatiable craving for the increase of God's glory, and the complete fulfilment of His will. This is agreeable to the teaching of

St. Basil, in his shorter Rule, where he asks what is meant by one fervent in spirit. He answers, such a one who, "with earnest desire, and insatiable craving, and persevering diligence, does the will of God, through the love of our Lord Jesus Christ, according to that of the Psalmist—'*In His commandments doth he take exceeding delight.*'"* And, in truth, this ardour, this hunger and thirst after justice, suffice of themselves to stir up and stimulate the soul to neglect nought that may ensure the due performance, throughout the day, of the purpose we made at rising.

St. Ignatius supplies three suggestions, as so many props, most suited and efficacious for maintaining this fervour. (1) To limit our resolution to a brief space of time, as from morning till noon, from noon till bedtime. (2) Frequently to renew our purpose. (3) Not to lose heart when we fall, but to gain courage from our very bruises, and to renew the conflict with more earnest resolutions. By these means, which should ever be accompanied by constant and fervent prayer, he assures us of winning the victory in the end.

To begin then, it will be of great avail for getting rid of the qualms and pusillanimity of the imagination, to limit the time of the struggle, and to confine our resolve to a brief space. Travellers to a great distance are wont to make use of this means; they know full well how to disguise the weariness of a long journey, by dividing it into easy stages, and by fixing their minds on a distance their eye can measure; thus do they manfully overcome fatigue,

* Q. 259.

and reach at length to the term, be it never so distant. Plutarch, a Pagan philosopher, bears witness that he thus succeeded in repressing the sallies of his vicious passions, and especially of anger. "This year," said he to himself, "I will be moderate in my drink; during this month, I will carefully keep from lying, even in joke; in the following month I will endeavour to practise patience, and to refrain from every angry word." He assures us that he found this method most advantageous. St. Ignatius, on this very account, breaks up the time into short intervals, in that he prescribes for each day a twofold self-examination in order to amend a single fault—one at noon, and the other in the evening, so that our resolution at rising extends but to noon, and that we make at noon goes no further than the evening, for he says—"*Having done thus much, he will renew his resolution to keep himself in check for the remainder of the day.*"

The practical application of this method demands that we should dismiss the past from our mind, and not forecast the future; that we consider ourselves as engaging in the conflict for the first time this very morning, and that it will come to a close at noon; that it recommences at noon to finish with the day. In order to this, we must not allow our memory to recur to bygones, and are to close our eyes to all that lies beyond the term prefixed, be it noon or night. For the thought of even half a day, if weighted with past and future troubles, were too heavy a load to be borne. Let each one renew himself, so to speak, daily, and start on the assumption that he now takes up this exercise for the first time, and that it is his first encounter with the foe. For most truly was it said by St. Gregory—" By the very fact of living, the fervour of our soul diminishes. . . . As a garment wears out by use, so that at length a new one is needed, so, too, our purpose and fervour slacken and grow vapid, unless renewed. The way of such renewal is to forget the things that are behind, and to stretch forward to what lies before us, precisely in the same manner as if we were now beginning."* Wherefore he observes further on—" The just persevere in a new life, for that they daily begin."† And elsewhere—" The soul that ever strives by its desire to begin anew, can never relax into torpor. Hence St. Paul warns us, *Be you renewed in the spirit of your mind.*' Hence, too, the Psalmist, though he had reached the summit of perfection, says, as one beginning, *'I said, now do I begin.*' For, of a truth, if we would not weary of our good undertakings, it is most needful that we daily look upon ourselves as beginners."‡ Thus far St. Gregory. The author of the *Imitation of Christ* writes in the same spirit—" Wherever we be, we ought to walk before Him, as pure as Angels. We must daily renew our purpose, and stir ourselves up to fervour, as if this were the first day of our conversion, and say, "O Lord God, assist me in my good purpose, in Thy holy service, and grant me to begin perfectly to-day, for what I have hitherto done is nought."§ For this self-renewal, and to avoid the weariness which may arise from the past,

* 10 *Morals, on Job* xxvii.   † *Ibid.*   ‡ *Morals,* iv.
§ Book i., chap. xix., n. i.

a consideration such as this will prove most effectual. To escape the disgust which the length of the future may occasion, as we imagine each day we renew our purpose to be the first, so may we think that it may also be our last. By this means our resolution will become more efficacious, as it is confined within shorter intervals. The *Imitation of Christ* contains the like observation, when it says—" We should make our resolution from festival to festival, as if we were then to pass out of the world in order to go to the everlasting festival." If it be asked how we may restrict our resolution to half a day, knowing full well that we shall have to keep it for our whole lives? we may answer, that you are not sure that the sun of your life will not set before this noon, or this very night. Happy the man who daily struggles as if he were that very day to bring his conflict to its term, and whom the end of life finds thus combatting. Granting that our life may be protracted to a greater length, what can better contribute, will I ask, to living aright, than to be earnest and diligent each day to improve it, and to lay aside the uncertain expectation of months and years to come? You will meet with many who wax fervent in order to sustain the conflict of one day, but who lose their energy if the conflict have to be renewed on the morrow.

At times they will not dare to face the chance of a wound to-day, because they foresee the disaster of the morrow. As if the foe they manfully withstand to-day will not be weaker to-morrow, or the gracious help they are now putting to such good use were to fail them then. Find me a man who will refuse bread offered him to-day, for fear of falling short on the morrow. Or who will not put on his garment now from the uncertainty he is in as to his getting another? Countless other instances may be alleged to put such cowardice to the blush. "*Be not careful for the morrow*," says Christ. The morrow may never dawn. But granting it will—"*The morrow shall care for itself. Sufficient for the day is the evil thereof.*"* If you load to-day with the toil of the morrow, take heed lest you fall beneath the burden. If Christ, in this very passage, forbids anxiety about food, raiment, and the needs of this life, for that our Father in Heaven will not allow such as seek the Kingdom of God to want them; how much more care will not our Father take to supply the necessaries of spiritual life to them that are earnest in seeking His Kingdom. If an earthly father forthwith gives the bread of this life to his child that asks him, "*How much more shall your Father from Heaven give the Holy Spirit to them that ask Him?*"† It is therefore plain, that though the purpose of this conflict have to be daily renewed, the battle must each day be fought as if the war were only then beginning, and as if nothing remained to be done after the coming noon or evening. The time of the battle being thus shortened, what craven will allow a few slight qualms to hinder his striving manfully?

But a resolution made on this plan still seems to labour under one disadvantage, in that being limited to so brief a space, it has no influence for the future

* St. Matt. vi. 34.   † St. Luke xi. 13.

that is beyond it. Now, this disadvantage, if it be one, is amply provided against by the frequent renewal of our resolution. St. Ignatius requires us to make our resolves in the morning as soon as we rise until noon, and again at noon for the remainder of the day. He does not, however, require us to make a fresh resolution at night, either because he refers us to the Fifth Point of the General Examen, taking for granted that every scrutiny of our faults must end in sorrow for them, and in a purpose of amendment; or because there seems to be no great necessity of renewing our purpose as sleep soon follows upon this examen, and that it may on that account be deferred to the time of rising. For, as in this struggle the devil can harm only such as are awake; to a valorous combatant in this arena it ought to be one and the same thing to awake from sleep and to arm himself anew with his resolution. During the course of the day there is no room for hesitation, but the end of the term of one purpose must be the beginning of another still more fervent one. St. Ignatius, to tell the truth, demands even more, to wit—that as often as we fail in our resolution during the day, we renew it by putting our hand to our breast and sorrowing for our fault. We find this in the first Addition. The first is, that as often as the person "*shall have committed a sin of this sort, placing his hand on his breast, he will be sorry for his fall, which may be done without being noticed by others present.*"

No special efficacy is assigned to this outward gesture, which serves but to move us to reflect in order to the acknowledgment and reparation of our fault, to warn us to make an act of sorrow, and outwardly to attest that we renew our resolution. These inward acts are of the greatest avail for the amendment of the fault we have committed, nor is the outward gesture without its use in helping us to make them inwardly; for no sooner do we fall and go astray, by that outward sign, as by a sort of penalty, do we compel ourselves to renew our good purpose. This renewal is wholly conformable to reason, and the need of it is proportionate to our frailty and to the frequency of our falls.

This diligence further shakes off torpor, and prevents us from turning our back on the object of our pursuit, though we be never so often driven back by passion or evil habit. For a fall cannot dishearten us if it afford us an occasion of strengthening our purpose. A certain longanimity is here requisite; and as we confine our resolution to short periods of time, so must we allow a long interval for the gaining of a complete victory. For he who writes —"In the morning resolve, at evening examine thy doings;"* also says—"If we were to uproot but one vice every year, we should soon become perfect men." † And elsewhere—"By slow degrees, by patience, and long-suffering (God helping), you will succeed better than by your own stubbornness and importunity." ‡ Whence it is obvious that the mid-day and evening examen do not mean that the whole undertaking can be completed in the space of a whole or half day, but that this care and diligence

---

* *Imitation*, book i., chap. xix., n. 4.
† *Ibid.*, chap. xi., n. 5.   ‡ *Ibid.*, chap. xiii., n. 4.

greatly contribute to your success. Still, however, you may deem yourself most lucky if you succeed in a year's time.

To conclude, let us hearken to St. John Chrysostom prescribing to habitual swearers a means of getting rid of that degrading custom: on the one hand, he requires intense and daily diligence; on the other, he inculcates great patience and courage even after a relapse. After having for many days feelingly spoken to the people of Antioch against this abuse, he says—"If after this you urge that it is difficult for habit not to take unawares even such as are on their guard, I grant it; but I add that it is no less easy to amend than to be surprised. For if at home you set many sentinels everywhere, as, for instance, your servant, wife, friends, being thus hedged in and restrained on every side, you will soon get rid of your evil custom. If you keep to this but for ten days, you will need it no further; but by courage all will be restored to you."* . . . "When therefore you set about amending this fault, whether you break your resolution once, twice, or thrice, or twenty times, do not lose heart, but rise again, resume your struggle, and you will surely be victorious." † Thus far St. John Chrysostom.

* *Homily to the People of Antioch*, xxviii.
† *Ibid.*, xcviii.

CHAPTER VII.

OF THE TIMES OF THIS EXAMEN, AND THE FOUR ADDITIONS CONCERNING IT.

FROM what we have heretofore said, it is obvious that the first step in this Examen is the desire and purpose of correcting some one defect, which, like a goodly flower watered by the dews of heavenly grace, and cherished by an outpouring from on high, begins to bud forth at early morn in the garden of the heart. In the course of the day we must be diligently careful to make the fruits of good works correspond with the flowers of holy desires. This will be greatly forwarded, if the morning resolution be frequently renewed and our endeavours be confined within a brief interval. Nor are we to relax in our efforts, however often our frailty or evil habits may cause us to relapse into the fault we have purposed to avoid. It remains, in order to the daily diminution of these defects, that we take an exact account of them at appointed times, and that with the Spouse, "*We get up early* (in due time and with all diligence) *to the vineyards, and see whether the vines flourish, whether the blossoms contain the tender grape.*"* St. Gregory, in his commentary on this passage, says: "The Spouse rises early to go to the vineyards; he sees whether the vines flourish, in that he takes strict account of all the progress of the Church." The care the Spouse has for the Church, which causes her to

* Cant. vii. 12.

inquire whether the desires inspired from on high bear fruit, is the care we should take of the vineyard of our soul. The method of this Examen is reduced to two points. (1) To take account of the faults committed from morning till noon, and to note their number in a book provided for that purpose. (2) To compare the sum total of the morning with that of the evening, which are to be set down likewise; to compare in like manner, day with day, week with week, month with month, to discover whether we are advancing, or falling back. St. Ignatius supposes us to have at hand a book, with two lines ruled for each day, or one equal in length to both, above which as many points are marked as we have committed faults in the forenoon, while underneath are to be set down those of the afternoon. And as these numbers may reasonably be expected to decrease, the lines are made to diminish in length. This is especially set forth by St. Ignatius, when, after the four Additions, he says—"*It may be seen from the following figures, that the longest line is set opposite the Sunday, or whatever day may be the first; the next, which is somewhat shorter, is for the Monday, and so on to the end, as it may reasonably be hoped that the number of faults will diminish.*" This is the method prescribed by St. Ignatius. We may make use of a different one, if it but be adapted to the ends which we have described above. This being presupposed, the method of this Examen differs not from that of the general examen, as St. Ignatius declares as follows—"*The second time is about noon, when he must beg of God grace to recall how often he has fallen into this particular sin, or fault, and to beware of it for the future. He then makes the Examen, calling his soul to account as to the sin or vice aforesaid, going through each portion of the bygone day, from the time of rising to the present, how often he has committed it, and then shall he make as many dots as there are faults on the upper line of the annexed table. Having performed this, he will renew his purpose, to restrain himself more carefully during the remainder of the day."* Such are the prescriptions of the sainted author, wherein, passing by the first point of the general examen, he briefly details the remaining four points of this examen. To these points he adds the noting down of the number of falls, as being most suitable to this exercise, and easy of practice with regard to a special defect, for in the general examen on all our faults it were difficult, not to say impossible. Toward night, the third time of this exercise, another examen is to be made, concerning which St. Ignatius says, "*The third time is the evening, at which, after supper, the second examen is to be made, by going in the same manner over every hour since the last examen to the present, recalling and counting in likewise the number of times he has failed, and setting down an equal number of dots on the lower line, as drawn in the annexed table, which is provided for that purpose.*"

We have two observations to make concerning this Examen. (1) It is not enough to seek out the number of our falls, but we should further see what has been the occasion thereof; nor is a mere purpose of amendment to be deemed sufficient, but we must seriously forecast these occasions of falling. The fruit of such inquiry will be not only to render us more cautious when the occasion recurs, but also to relieve the monotony of this examen, by a search into the occasion of our transgressions, and into the remedies thereof, which we must effectually arrive at. (2) As the examen is preceded by a petition for light, and followed by contrition, or sorrow for the faults discovered to us by the examen, both the preliminary prayer, and the compunction which follows, will avail as much, nay even more, than the examen itself to make us gain a knowledge of our faults. Not that this ought to induce us to neglect, or to make little account of the examen, but rather to avoid the example of some who make it without asking for light, and without an act of sorrow. For both of these contribute to render the examen more easy, and give an increase of light, and bear more abundant fruit. For compunction opens the eyes of the mind, and prayer brings light. But this prayer requires a soul at peace, and devoid of passion, while compunction supposes a humble soul distrustful of self, as we have before observed. They both raise the soul above itself, so that being illumined with a ray of light from above, it may discover whatever lurks within the heart. Then will it no longer seek to palliate or excuse its shortcomings, but rather on discovering them will it be its own accuser. This is a lesson given by St. Gregory the Great, who treating of the necessity of examining into our virtues and faults (of the latter, lest they disguise themselves under the mask of virtue; of the former, lest they degenerate into vice), proceeds to say, "These virtuous affections are more easily won by prayer than by self-examination. For the things we strive to discover within ourselves by self-questioning, we ofttimes more clearly penetrate by supplication than by research. The mind being lifted on high by means of compunction gains a more certain insight into whatever may be presented as concerning itself, by looking down upon it from a higher level." Thus far St. Gregory. Further considerations on this preliminary prayer are to be found in the treatise on the General Examen.

In the second place, we are to compare and set in contrast the faults we have committed at different times, a practice which is especially appropriate to the Particular Examen. On this head, St. Ignatius subjoins the three following additions—" *The second is that having at night-time counted and compared the points on either line, the upper one of which belongs to the first, and the lower to the second examen, he will see whether in the interval between these two examens there has been any amendment. The third is to compare together the examens of the first and the following day, in order to find out what amendment has been attained. The fourth is, by comparing the results of two weeks with each other to take account of the amendment made, or not made.*" This requires rather to be put into practice than to be explained, nor could a more exact instruction for such a purpose be imagined, or one more conformable to the maxims of the ancient Fathers on this point. For St. Bernard exhorts his Monks as follows, "The present day must be compared with the foregoing one, in order to discover by such comparison, one's progress, or backsliding." The

Mirror for Monks, towards the end, and Dorotheus, in like manner says (Doctrine 10, at the end), "We must examine ourselves not only every day, but every season, every month, every week; and say to ourselves, The first week of this month thou wast addicted to such a vice, how art thou now? Thus should we diligently seek out whether we still wallow in the same depths, or whether we have fallen still lower." St. Basil, in his turn, "Recall to thyself towards evening thy doings during the bygone day, and set them side by side with those of the preceding one. And strive diligently to improve daily."*

* *Sermon on Renouncement.*

CHAPTER VIII.

THE EFFICACY OF THIS EXAMEN.

NONE may question the efficacy of this examen when duly made according to the instructions of our holy Founder, St. Ignatius. Apart from the advantages resulting equally from the General and from the Particular Examen, its main virtue consists in our directing all our inquiries and endeavours against one particular vice we would be rid of. They who are overburdened with debt, without caring to pay, or to lower their style of living, though they are wasting their estate, and gradually sinking into beggary, are vehemently averse from looking into their accounts, avoid all knowledge of their debts, lest poverty, which is at their side, should present itself to their consideration and meet their gaze. While thus wilfully shutting their eyes to their incumbrances, they can fancy themselves rich, and flatter themselves that others deem them such, though it be not the fact; and as their burden increases, they with their creditors, at length, sink under it. Their sole chance of forestalling ruin, is to put their accounts in order, to examine them daily, and by judicious retrenchment to liquidate their obligations. Their heedlessness fittingly represents that of a spiritual man who makes no use of this Particular Examen. He shrinks from thus searching into his conscience, for that he is afraid to see himself as he is, he prefers that his faults should pass unnoticed; he deems himself religious, making some outward profession of virtue, yet to him applies the rebuke once addressed to the Bishop of Laodicea, "*Thou sayest, I am rich, and I have become wealthy, and have need of nothing; and knowest not that thou of all others art the wretched one, and the pitiable one, and poor, and blind, and naked.*" *

Let us then rest assured that the groundwork of all self-amendment is the knowledge of our shortcomings. For how shall that be reformed which is excused, palliated, carefully covered up, and of which we are ignorant? On the other hand, it is impossible but that one should set in earnest about his self-improvement who searches into his faults, numbers, and sets them down, comparing day with day, week with week. What can he feel but confusion who with holy David is able to say—"*My sin is ever before me*"?† We must set about amending ourselves in the same way as we strive to bring others back to good. We begin by convincing them of their faults. We then convict, exhort, and rebuke, according to the counsel of the Apostle—"*Preach the word, be urgent in season, out of season, convict, exhort, rebuke in all long-suffering and teaching.*"‡ Would you know when you are to rebuke? The Apostle makes answer—*In season, out of season.* Would you be told what this means? St. Chrysostom, in his *Homily* on this Epistle, replies—"What means in season, out of season, in due time, and out of due time? This: have no fixed time, let every moment be the proper time for you; not only that of calm and peace, or

---

* Apoc. iii. 17.
† Psalm l.   ‡ 2 Tim. iv. 2.

when you are sitting in the church, but amid perils, whether you be bound in prison, or laden with fetters, or, when doomed to death, you are being hurried to the scaffold; shrink not, at such times, from convicting, rebuking. . . . If you rebuke without proofs, you will be deemed over hasty, no one will bear with you. But when guilt is brought home to the culprit, he will more easily submit to rebuke, else he will be dead to shame. If you convict and rebuke passionately, and omit exhortation, you will undo everything. For by itself rebuke is unbearable, unless tempered by exhortation. Like as a sick man will not bear the surgeon's knife unless it assuage his pain, neither will your erring brother." These prescriptions of St. Chrysostom concern, indeed, the correction of our neighbour, yet are they no less suited to self-correction, in that they include the three points of the Examen. (1) A palpable self-conviction of one's faults by comparing day with day. (2) Rebuke, to stir up sorrow and shame. (3) Exhortation, by consideration exciting to confidence, whereby the purpose of amendment is strengthened. It were well to observe at this point, the way wherein God is wont to bring the sinner back to Himself, as we should make use of the self-same in our own case. Hear what God does—"*But to the wicked saith God: What hast thou to do to tell My precepts, and that thou hast taken My covenant into thy mouth? Whereas for thee, thou hatest instruction, and hast cast My words behind thee: when thou sawest a robber, thou consentedst with him, and with adulterers has been thy portion.*" After the enumeration of other sins, He continues—"*These things hast thou done, and for that I kept silence."* On that account—*"Thou thoughtest falsely, that I was like thyself; but I will rebuke thee, and lay the matter in order before thine eyes."** Which shows that seeming to take no notice of sin, and delaying its punishment, encourages the sinner not to enter into himself, as if God felt no displeasure at sins which He does not forthwith chastise, whence he is emboldened to take delight in his crimes. In like manner does our inferior man give full swing to his vices when reason winks at his excesses, and blindfolds itself lest it see them. For this the only remedy is that which God threatens—*"I will rebuke thee, and lay thy sins in order before thine eyes."* St. Augustine, in his Comments on this text, says—"For that I refrained from vengeance, put off My severity, and with redoubled patience waited long for thy repentance, *Thou thoughtest falsely that I was like thyself.* It is not enough for thee to take delight in thy sins, but thou must deem them pleasing to Me. Not feeling God's vengeance, thou wouldst hold Him for thy accomplice, for a partial Judge, for thy boon companion. *I will rebuke thee.* And what shall I do *thereby?* At present thou art hidden from thyself, but I will show thee to thyself. For didst thou see thyself and wert thou displeased with thyself, thou wouldst be pleasing unto Me. But for that not seeing thyself, thou art content with thyself, thou shalt be displeasing both to Me and to thee; to Me when thou shalt come to judgment, to thee when thou art burning. For what is it I shall do to thee, *but set thee before thy face.* Thou wouldst

---
* Psalm xlix. 16.

hide from thyself, thou hast turned thy back on thyself, but I will show thee thyself, and set before thy face what is now behind thy back. Thou shalt behold thy filthiness, not to cleanse it, but to be put to shame." Thus does St. Augustine apply this passage to God's rebuke of the wicked at the last day. He then continues—"Is he, then, to whom these things are said to despair? In nowise. Do thou, whoever thou art, do to thyself what God here threatens. Cease to turn thy back upon thyself, hiding from thine own eyes, set thee before thyself. Go up to the judgment-seat of thy conscience, let fear terrify thee, let confession break forth from thy lips, say unto thy God—'*For I know my transgressions, and my sin is ever before me.*'" The holy Doctor takes God's judgment as a model of that we should exercise upon ourselves in this life, and shows that the first step to conversion is the knowledge of our faults and of the injury they do to us. Now such knowledge is the fruit of this Examen.

In conclusion, we may observe that among the rules laid down for this self-examination, some are essential, the very soul, so to speak, of this Examen, and these are the inward acts of the mind, as, for instance, the morning resolution, the careful and watchful passing of the day, the inquiry, at regular times, into the number of our falls, contrition, and purpose of amendment, the comparison of different periods, so as to take account of one's improvement. In these does the very essence of this Exercise consist. Other details, though not indispensable, yet are useful as helping to make the Examen more easy, and to expedite improvement; such are the outward actions of laying our hand on our breast when we fall, of noting our faults in a book, of comparing the morning and evening account, that of to-day with yesterday's, &c. These form the body of this Exercise, and enable us to set our falls before our eyes, and to feel with our hands, as it were, their diminution. This is no recent invention, but long since in use among those who strove earnestly for their advancement. John Climacus, in his *Spiritual Ladder*, writes as follows—"Perceiving that a Brother carried hanging to his girdle a small book, I got to know that he daily set down his thoughts therein, and was wont to give account of them to his Prelate. He was not, by a good many, the only one whom I saw practise this in that monastery. I learned that it was a rule imposed on them by their ghostly Father."* Further on—" He is a most clever banker who daily at eventide takes account of his gains and losses, which cannot be done with accuracy unless they be hourly set down on tablets. For when entries are made every hour, the day's account is easily balanced." Whoso takes this method of uprooting his defects cannot fail of the victory.

For this unwearying, unintermittent diligence is of such avail, that it must needs work a change in a soul sunk in the grossest and most inveterate evil habits, uproot sin, and implant virtue. In truth, it will more readily enable those whom the rebellion of nature has subjected to heinous faults, to scale the summit of perfection, if they will but persevere therein, than

* Degree 4, on Obedience.

milder, more pliable, and gentler characters, who are less energetic and diligent in watching over themselves. Most truly it is stated in the *Imitation of Christ*—"He that is diligent and earnest, though he have more passions to fight against, will be able to make greater progress than another with fewer passions, but withal less fervent in the pursuit of virtue."*

Thus much concerning the method of this Examen, now pass we to its matter.

* Book i., chap. xxv., n. 4.

CHAPTER IX.

THE MATTER OF THE PARTICULAR EXAMEN.

THIS vast field may be mapped out into three subdivisions. The first is the sin, fault, or aught else we wish to amend. To this head may be reduced whatever regards our more or less depraved natural propensities, whatever is sinful and opposed to the divine law, to the rules, orders, and duties of one's state or condition. Our holy Founder has expressly taught this kind of method, in that he headed his four Additions with this title—*Additions useful for the more easy and speedier uprooting of whatsoever sin or vice.* It must be borne in mind that sin or evil habits can be overcome, either directly by repressing them, and withdrawing or repelling that to which our propensity, passion, or evil habit inclines us, or indirectly, by the practice of the opposite virtue; and this forms the second subdivision, to wit, the exercise of virtue. But our vices must first be put away before we apply ourselves to the acquirement of virtue. The husbandman first cleans his field of nettles, briars, and noxious weeds, ere he scatters over it the good seed; in like manner, he who tills the field of his heart should begin by destroying his vices, and then apply himself to fostering the goodly growth of virtues, which may not only bring forth the fruit of holiness, but may in a more excellent way check the undergrowth of vice. The difference between these two methods is this: the former, aiming as it does at the extirpation of sin, is for beginners, the latter for proficients and the perfect. Beginners usually suffer from the hinderances these thorns put in their way; wherefore they must first begin by clearing them off ere they sow the seeds of virtue, according to the warning of Jeremias—"*Sow not among thorns.*"* This being accomplished, the Examen is to be applied to progress in virtue, in order that our vices may be more utterly overlaid, and that the soul may be disposed to the highest grade of charity, which surpasses all else.

We may now readily see what reply can be given to those who ask why St. Ignatius in treating of this Examen, appoints sins and evil habits as its matter, omitting virtues. This most able master imitates herein him who would put a wayfarer into the right road. He gives him clear directions as to his outset, but leaves it to the traveller's care to keep to the path marked out for him. Now the first step in the way of the spirit is to struggle against our vices. To this, then, does our master teach us to direct our gaze, without making mention of virtue, lest perchance he should mislead his disciples into beginning where they ought to end. The conflict with vice is more trying than the easy and far more pleasant pursuit of virtue, and this might lure a beginner into entering upon a path better suited to proficients and the perfect. The more so as the method of the Examen is in both cases alike, whether its matter be a vice or a virtue, so that he who knows how to use it against vice, needs no

* Jer. iv. 3.

one to direct him in its use when a virtue is its subject-matter. For, as when a vice is in question we must make our resolution each morning to guard against it, sum up the number of our falls, compare day with day, &c., the same method is to be followed with a virtue; we make our resolution, we take account of the number of times we have failed to keep it, &c. So that in either case the Examen is an inquiry into our shortcomings, whether it be a fall into sin, or a want of fidelity to our good purpose: in both cases there is obviously a fault. Lastly, our holy Father expressly teaches us how to apply this Examen to our Spiritual Exercises (the third subdivision of this vast field) by taking note of our failures in observing the additions and instructions, and of our exactness in fulfilling each duty at the appointed time and hour. The same method will serve equally for this third category. So that the three heads of this Examen are the uprooting of vice, the acquirement of virtue, the exact fulfilment of our spiritual duties. St. Ignatius prescribes that this last point be taken as the subject-matter of our Particular Examen, throughout the four weeks of the Spiritual Exercises, which, as will be noticed further on, is to be done at other times as well, seeing that the increase of virtue, and the subduing of our vices, and the prosperous growth of Christian justice within us, depends on the perfection wherewith we perform our spiritual duties. Passing by, for the present, this third arena of the Particular Examen, we will say somewhat concerning the conflict with vice, and the acquiring of virtue. The first maxim to be borne in mind is that we must aim but at one vice, and strive after one virtue, as is implied in the very name of this Examen. Division diminishes our strength, while union increases it. And as a general, when invading a kingdom, does not scatter his forces in besieging many towns at once, but keeps them united in order to invest one at a time, and when he has reduced it, leaving a garrison therein, he lays siege to another; so too should he act who sets about subduing his vices. He must encounter but one enemy at a time, and the most formidable one to begin with, as is well said by Abbot Serapion, in chapter xiv. of Cassian's fifth *Conference*, "We must wage war in this fashion, each one after examining to what vice he is most prone will direct his chief efforts against it, will apply with all care and diligence, and fix his whole attention on opposing it; at this will he aim the darts of his daily fastings, against it will he every moment hurl the javelins of his deep drawn sighs and moanings; against this will he direct the travail and meditations of his heart, and pouring forth with God his prayers and tears, he will earnestly beseech Him for the happy termination of this conflict." We may further learn this from what we read of God's plan for introducing His people into the land promised to their fathers. He would not have them to drive their foes before them in a single year, but step by step, that we might learn in what manner our vices and spiritual enemies are to be overcome. "*I will not drive them out from before thee in one year, saith the Lord. By little and little will I drive them out, until thou be increased. I will send hornets before thee, which shall drive out the Hevite, the Canaanite, and the Hethite before thou come in.*"* Again, "*Thou didst send wasps, forerunners of Thine host, to destroy them little by little.*"† What could better suit our subject? For the scruples and prickings of conscience which are wont to work much disturbance to those that strive after virtue, what else are they, but swarms of hornets and wasps torturing with their stings those who are resolved to wage war upon their vices? These insects destroying our inward peace, seem to war against the sinner himself; but it is against his vices they are sent. The power of sin consists in an appearance of somewhat delectable and good, wherewith, as with a bait, reason is lured to a headlong plunge, but when perplexity of conscience gives the soul to taste the bitterness lurking under this sweetness—a bitterness ingrained in sin, but which escapes observation—the soul, wincing under these goads, abhors its past deeds, is spurred on to do battle with the foes it has heretofore favoured, and makes effort to drive them off as far as possible. This is accomplished best by degrees; it is not the work of a single day, or month. Meanwhile, the man is strengthened in spirit, he gathers into his soul virtues, which as a garrison keep guard, and take the place vacated by his former sins. Where gluttony erst held sway, temperance now rules; meekness is enthroned in the place of anger; mercy and open handedness in that of covetous greed; chastity in that of profligacy; courage in lieu of pusillanimity; and pride, which is mixed up with all sins, now yields the place to humility. Thus is every vice eradicated by degrees, when we combine all our efforts against

* Exodus xxiii. 28, 29, 30.   † Wisdom xii. 8.

a single foe, and by the same means are all virtues made to flourish, but as was said we must direct our endeavours to one vice or virtue at a time. I add, moreover, that not only should we aim at the destruction of a single vice, or the acquirement of one virtue, but further, we ought to divide and subdivide such vice or virtue, according to its divers good or evil fruits, which spring from it as so many branches from a stock. Take pride as an instance: it predominates in arrogant thoughts, in boastful words, in pompous actions; on the other hand humility casts it out by its works, in that it seeks the lowest place in words, in that it owns to its shortcomings in thought by a lowly esteem of itself, and a readiness to meet every humiliation. This holds good of every vice or virtue. He, then, that would gather more abundant fruit, let him divide the several branches of the same tree; in this wise will his attention be less distracted, and his faults more easily numbered, as the matter is more sharply defined, since the force and efficacy of this Examen mainly consists in reflecting on our faults, in counting and comparing them together. Whatever else renders these operations more complete, contributes, moreover, to the perfection of this exercise.

CHAPTER X.

IN REPLY TO CERTAIN OBJECTIONS TO THE ABOVE.

THIS single combat is far from safe, nay, it is even perilous. For we are unceasingly assailed on all sides by so many vices, that if we employ all the energies of our soul in the conflict with one, we are in danger of being overcome by the others. Judas Machabeus met with disaster from having divided his forces, for while with his bravest troops he threw himself upon the right wing of the enemy, which was far the stronger, and routed it, another portion of his army was put to flight by the enemy, and being attacked in the rear by the victorious foe, Judas and his soldiers were slain.* Who should not dread his sad fate, if he employ all his energies against one only vice, and that the most powerful? But they who are practised in this spiritual warfare are little moved by this objection. They are well aware that they cannot thus fight against one vice without attacking all, and that a complete victory over this one enemy is the undoing of the rest of the conspirators. As one virtue acquired in perfection cannot be kept without drawing all the others in its train, wherefore may we infer that among the several means for speedy progress in perfection, the Particular Examen may claim the first place. This will appear beyond question if we but look to its matter, method, and actual accompaniments. Its matter are our vices,

* 1 Mach. ix. 12.

especially that which predominates within us, and is the head of all the rest. Now as all vices hold more or less together, and afford each other reciprocal aid in order to obtain the rule over our hearts, like as in drawing one link of a chain the whole chain is drawn, so, likewise, he who declares truceless war against one vice, thereby resists all others, and all are involved in the overthrow of one enemy. And this applies still more to the case of a vice which is the leader of all the others. To make this plain by an example, let us take covetousness, or love of money, as an instance of a predominant vice. Every other is subservient to it as to its lord. Pride makes little or no account of what it already possesses. Injustice puts forth its hand to another's goods. Envy grudges its neighbour his gains. Anger chafes at the obstacles to one's own profits—and so on of other vices. Now if all vices do thus take up arms in defence of that which is their head, it is plain that when this latter is overthrown, all the others must needs totter to their fall. He who attacks a monster with many feet and hands, but with one head, will not aim at these several members, if he can but strike at the head, which if once severed gives him a complete victory. In like manner, arduous and bootless strength is wasted in the conflict with vices unless we aim at the head of them the deadly blow which will make us victorious over all the others. Of this the Syrian monarch was well aware when he ordered his soldiers —"*Fight neither with small nor great*, save only with the King of Israel."* In like manner in the war

---

* 3 Kings xxii. 31.

waged by the Jews against the Philistines, when David had struck off Goliath's head, he put the hosts of the foe to rout—"*And when the Philistines saw their champion was dead, they fled.*"* In looking, then, to the subject-matter of this Examen, it is obvious that this one vice is so closely connected with the rest of its crew, that it is impossible to slay one and to overlook the others so as to lay ourselves open to their attacks, but that it is the same thing as assailing them all, and that victory over one means the overthrow of the rest.

This becomes plainer still if we look to the method, which is to make our resolution on rising, and to keep watch and ward throughout the day, lest the foe find any hole to creep through. Our carefulness not to fall into this vice will help us to avoid vice in general. The common well-spring of all of them is the indulgence we show to our lusts and appetites. As the Holy Ghost says—"*Go not after thy lusts, and refrain thyself from thine appetites. If thou givest thy soul the desires that please her, she will make thee a laughing-stock to thine enemies.*"† If, then, the liberty allowed to our lusts is the common root of every vice, the restraint we subject it to cannot but serve to their correction. Wherefore he that makes his Examen on one only vice, say of look, or of speech, and seriously proposes to curtail its vagaries, restrains his appetite in other matters too. When an unruly horse rushes over hill and dale, if he be bitted and bridled, he will in all things follow the lead of his rider. The same holds good of our irregular

* 1 Kings xvii. 52.   † Ecclus. xviii. 30, 31.

appetites when we apply ourselves to this Examen. For though we hold our lusts in check with a view to one vice, we learn at the same time to subdue the others, and to yield obedience to reason and the divine law. This may be instanced in another way. If a man go armed against one enemy laying in wait for him, although he have taken arms to defend himself against his one foe, he will be no less secured against any other enemy who may chance to assail him. The like holds good of him who, arming himself at early morn with a steadfast purpose and an earnest will against a certain vice, calling at the same time on God for help, lest he falter. All this he does with a view to a single vicious habit, yet is he wonderfully helped thereby should he be assailed by a vice of another description.

This becomes still more obvious if we look into the purpose and the accompaniments of this Examen. Its purpose is to subdue vice, to ensure cleanness of heart, and the fulfilment of God's law. Its chief help is God's grace, which we strive to obtain by fastings, austerities, watching, prayers, and tears, as Abbot Serapion taught us heretofore. If I take such trouble to keep my heart undefiled by one vice, who may deem that I shall be a craven and yield to another temptation whereby the purity I so anxiously desire will be no less sullied? He who girds his sword to ward off the strokes of one who thirsts for his blood, will not shrink from drawing it if an unexpected foe attempt his life. The love of dear life will be equally efficacious in both cases. He who is neat and particular, and makes up his mind to go cautiously to avoid the mud, lest he soil his shoes, is not likely to throw himself into a place where he will befoul his coat. His love of neatness will make him beware of both. So, likewise, as spiritual life, innocency of soul, and the fulfilment of the divine will, are the end and aim of this Examen, and urge the soul to avoid a single vice, it cannot be but they will urge her to avoid whatever is repugnant to this end. But what shall we say of the means which serve to compass this end? Of the desires, prayers, tears, austerities made use of for the same purpose? Can they who are determined to take such pains in order to rid themselves of one vice, be careless of pleasing the Divine Majesty in other matters, or make no account of offending Him? Courtiers who aspire to some favour or post of dignity strive to make themselves pleasing not only to the King, from whom alone they can hope to obtain the desired gift, but sparing no pains to be agreeable to the Ministers whom they know to be able to further their wishes. On the same account do they endeavour to win the divine approval in all things who are resolved, His grace helping, to root out some one vice, or to acquire a certain virtue. They aspire, indeed, but to the courage to face vice, yet are they well aware that they cannot compass this if they allow themselves to be overcome in other matters.

It remains but to establish the doctrine we have thus unfolded so fully by the authority of the aforementioned Serapion, who continues the quotation alleged above as follows—" Nor may we fancy that he who is mainly intent on combatting a single vice, and takes no heed of the darts of the others, is likely to be struck with an unforeseen blow; it is in nowise the case. For it cannot be that one who of his care for the amendment of his inner man, applies his mind to the subduing of any one vice, should not feel a general abhorrence for all the others, and guard himself against them. For how shall he deserve to obtain the victory over the vice he desires to be rid of who renders himself unworthy, by the defilement of other vices, of the purity he aspires to?"

CHAPTER XI.

THE MANNER AND ORDER OF CHOOSING THE MATTER OF THE PARTICULAR EXAMEN.

ORDER, so important in any affair whatsoever, is most essential in spiritual concerns. He who builds a house must do all things in a settled order, the foundations have to be dug and examined, before erecting the walls and covering the roof. If it be neglected in the culture of the spirit, our labour is in vain. Hence so many, after years of prayer and austerities, make scarce any progress. To set this point in a proper light, I will lay down the following instructions:

The matter of this Examen being, as we have said, threefold, to wit, vices, virtues, and our spiritual exercises, whenever we are in retreat, and have no other object but to gather fruit from the Spiritual Exercises, we may make this Examen with a view to ensure the utmost exactness in the performance of these exercises, either according to the rules set us by our director, or, if we be experienced in this matter, according to a method we may set forth for ourselves. We must keep to this during the whole course of the Exercises, as St. Ignatius lays it down at the end of the tenth Addition of the first week. Having completed the Exercises, if beginners, we must choose some one vice to be rooted out, others will select a virtue they will endeavour to acquire. It must further be remembered that in all these matters there are acts of different kinds; some inward, which remain in the mind and heart, and others outwards, forming, as it were, a visible body for the former ones. Such are words, deeds, occasions, outward motions, the acts of the senses. A few examples will make this clear. In pride we have haughty thoughts, boastful words, ambitious deeds; in envy, sad thoughts at our neighbour's success, grumbling speeches at his good fortune, deeds tending to his disadvantage. In humility, on the contrary, we meet with lowly thoughts, disposing one to put up with injury, &c, words of self-depreciation, deeds of submission, and so on of the other virtues and vices. So, too, in the Spiritual Exercises, are there certain outward actions, in which they are, so to speak, embodied, such as a reverent posture in time of prayer, presence at the Divine Office and other pious exercises, hearing Mass, spending one's time in meditations and examens, in such bodily and mental posture as bespeaks attention and earnestness. The inward acts lie invisible in the three powers of the soul; they are diligent meditation and fervent affections.

This being taken for granted, the second instruction is that in these several matters the Examen should never begin with the merely spiritual acts, for that these acts easily escape our scrutiny, even were we deeply versed in spiritual experiences, and our mind is so unstable and wavering that it is scarce conscious to the full of its own thoughts. It is also frequently the case that these thoughts and emotions are not voluntary and free, but proceed from mere spontaneity. Hence they who are not well grounded in spiritual things will be unable to determine whether or no they be faulty, so that, when the number of falls has to be counted, everything becomes mixed up with anxieties and scruples. Besides which, there is no small difficulty in correcting these defects, for our inward acts do not so entirely depend on the control of the will as not to take us continually by surprise, even in despite of ourselves. We ofttimes have thoughts we would well be rid of; and, for all we may strive, it is not altogether in our power to banish these thoughts. We at times will what we would not, nor does the jarring of conflicting affections cease but with life itself, as St. Paul fully experienced.* For as one must be an able horseman to mount an unruly horse which cannot brook restraint, so the task of reducing our inward acts to perfect order must be left to those who have long dwelt with themselves, and are skilled in observing the workings of the inner man. Better by far is it to make a beginning with outward actions, which, being more under the control of the will, are more easily governed, more readily discerned in all the circumstances wherein they fall short of the rule of right reason. Obedience, for instance, requires ready compliance, even so as to leave a letter unfinished. It further demands the inward submission of the will and judgment. So many difficulties beset this latter point for beginners that they cannot themselves say when they have fallen and when they rise from their fall. The first point is far otherwise; they are able to put their

* Rom. vii. 19.

finger, so to speak, on their failures, and, as it is wholly dependent on the will, they may easily know the exact number of their faults, and promise themselves a speedy victory.

Two other reasons may be alleged in support of this view. (1) Outward defects give scandal, detract from the estimation of virtue in the eyes of our neighbour, and hence call for speedy correction. (2) Although our failings have their root within, in the soul, the correction of the outward actions tends to weaken this root. Thus, if the high opinion I have of myself makes me utter haughty words, the checking of these words reaches to the heart, and represses the sentiment which finds its expression in them. If my soul chafe under the yoke of obedience, its insubordination is kept in check by the ready performance of what is commanded. Thus does the war we wage with our outward failings tell upon those that lurk within.

The third instruction is that, amongst outward actions, deeds are to be amended before words, and this because when our thoughts are translated not only into words but into deeds, we have a sign of a deep-rooted habit, and of greater deliberation in the will, on which account a speedy remedy is required; and we must apply the remedy to the part which is most grievously wounded. It is obvious that sins of deed are more heinous than the others, for a threefold reason, as St. Ignatius teaches in the General Examen—"*On account of the greater length of time, the greater intensity of the act, the injury or scandal done to many more persons.*" Faults of speech, on the contrary, take less time, pre-suppose less deliberation, and do not indicate so deeply-rooted a passion. The tongue most readily follows the mind, and resembles the hands of a clock. It beats, so to speak, responsive to every emotion of the heart, and moves almost as swiftly as the thoughts of the mind. Wherefore it is more advisable to correct words before thoughts, as they are more under the control of reason, but, for the reasons stated above, beginners will find it most easy to begin with deeds.

CHAPTER XII.

FURTHER INSTRUCTIONS ON THE SAME SUBJECT.

WE have now to determine what order is to be kept in singling out our vices—on which of them we should make the first onslaught. For clearness' sake we will observe that vices may be considered in their nature or with regard to the disposition of the subject. Further, some vices may be called spiritual, because, like moths, they breed within the soul; such are pride, vanity. While others are carnal, as proceeding from carnal lusts and the appetites of the body, as gluttony, profligacy, &c. The fourth instruction, then, is that, if we consider our vices in themselves, those who have been the slaves of sensual excess, and are troubled rather by carnal than spiritual passions, should begin by mortifying their sensuality, in that it is to them a source of more pressing danger, without making any account of the temptations to vainglory which may arise from their efforts, and detract from the purity of their intention, provided they can but subdue their more powerful foes, from whom they have the most to fear, and subject them to the control of reason. Serapion, in Cassian's *Conferences*, is of the same opinion, for he holds that at times we shall do well to avail ourselves of the help of a spiritual vice, in order to overcome the defilements of the flesh. These are his words—"Vainglory may prove of advantage to beginners in one case—to such as are still subject to the incentives of the vice of the flesh. For instance, if, when molested by the spirit of uncleanness, they were to turn their minds to the priestly dignity, or to their general repute for a holy and blameless life, they might deaden the stings of lust, as vile or unworthy of that order, or incompatible with their fair fame, thus overcoming a greater evil by one which is less. For better is it that one should be tempted to vainglory than that he should fall into the furnace of fornication, whence he may never be rescued, or be rescued but after a fatal fall." Thus far the holy Abbot. And in truth, though vice may not claim our approval, yet it may be so far forth useful, inasmuch as it serves to hinder a greater evil, and may suggest motives against falling which avail more with the imperfect than any others. It is surely better to be wounded than to be killed; and further, a care for one's good name may be worthy of praise. It may therefore be taken as certain that he who is liable both to carnal and spiritual ailments, should begin with the former, as being more scandalous and injurious.

The fifth instruction is to keep the following order in dealing with the vices of the flesh, to turn our arms against gluttony first. It was not without a well-considered purpose that St. Ignatius, in his Spiritual Exercises, gives the first place among the rules to those entitled "On Moderation in Eating." It is a well-known maxim of the *Imitation*—"Bridle gluttony, and thou shalt more easily restrain all fleshly appetites."* And St. Basil most truly calls gluttony the fertile seed-plot of every vice. "Like as a fountain of

* Book i., chap. 19, n. 4.

water, if distributed into many channels, clothes with verdure the spots bordering on the several streamlets, and makes them to flourish, so if the vice of gluttony spread itself through the veins of thy heart, and welling up therefrom, overflow thy senses, after having sown within the seeds of countless lusts, it will change thy soul into a den of wild beasts."* He proceeds to say that gluttony makes its slaves to spurn the calling to a higher life, and leads many to desert religion. "The first temptation," says Cassian, "of gluttony, is to hurry to take refreshment before the appointed and regular time. The next is to delight in filling one's belly, and in our eagerness to partake of whatever is set before us. The third is to seek for dainties. The first begets hatred of the monastery, which, in its turn, grows into an abhorrence and disgust, soon to be followed by desertion, or flight." St. Basil confirms this teaching, for he continues— "Many have I met with, who, though subject to vices of another kind, recovered their health later on. But of those who were enslaved to gluttony, so as to find a satisfaction in secret repasts, or to yield to the cravings of the belly, I have never known one to reform. For they either separated themselves from the fellowship of those who observed continency, and plunged without remorse into the sinful delights of this life, or if they sought to lurk among such, they indulged their appetites, and did service to the devil." Thus far St. Basil. The battle, then, must begin with gluttony. Next come incontinency and the sins of the flesh. Thirdly, covetousness, or greed of gain.

* *On the renouncement of all things.*

Fourthly, anger. Fifthly, melancholy; and lastly, sloth. These several vices are so closely connected together, that if the first in order prevail over us, the others are sure to follow in its wake. For gluttony begets impurity, impurity covetousness, covetousness anger, anger melancholy, melancholy sloth. Wherefore the order of attack must correspond with that of these vices. It is less troublesome to pull up the root than to lop the branches off; if the fountain be stopped, the brook soon dries up.

CHAPTER XIII.

EXAMPLES OF EACH VICE TO ILLUSTRATE THE DIVISION OF THE EXAMEN.

WE have thus set forth the order of attack; we have shown that the vices are to be divided into parts, according to which division we must begin with deeds, proceed next to words, and then to thoughts. It remains but to set forth examples of a fitting division, so as to pave the way to an advantageous selection.

§ I. *Instances of Gluttony.*—(1) Not to eat out of time, or anticipate the hour of meals, or to eat in any but the usual place; to taste of nothing without leave. (2) To abstain from all dainties, or anything peculiar, without a real necessity; to forego the sumptuous repasts of worldlings, when it can be done without giving offence; to feel ashamed, should it befall us to taste aught for the mere gratification of the palate. (3) To partake of common food in moderation, never to repletion; not to empty the dish set before us, but to leave some morsel, and one which we would relish most. (4) To abstain from wine (especially in youth) unless necessity compel; to avoid fine wines, liquors, &c.; to be content with the diet of the poor. (5) Not to speak of tasty or unsavoury food; the same, also, of drink. Never to converse about such things. For as it is unbecoming to be guided by our taste while eating, it is still more so to speak about this matter after our meals. (6) Not to anticipate the gratification of eating before meals, or to feed the mind while at table, but at such to entertain some pious thought as is prescribed in the rules for *Moderation in Eating*.

§ II. *Instances of Lust.*—(1) To banish far from oneself deeds of darkness and shamelessness. (2) To keep one's touch undefiled, even with one's own body; for a coal, when lighted, burns; when quenched, it blackens. (3) Not to touch another, either on the head, on the face, hands, clothes, whether in play, or friendship. The embraces given to new comers, and to those that are taking leave, should be unaffected, redolent of chastity. (4) As with the touch, so, too, must the eyes be averted from every nude and indecent representation; and where such may be met with, they must be held in check. (5) One should avoid familiarity with the opposite sex, by long conversations, letters, presents, by fixedly looking at them. In all these points, one should rigorously bind oneself never to be without a companion as a witness, and to report to the Superior when necessity requires. (6) One must abstain from witty and trifling words, keep from books treating of lascivious matters. (7) Every impure thought is to be at once stamped out like a spark; nor should we presume on our virtue, knowing full well that our flesh, like tow or gunpowder, readily catches the baleful flame. Lastly, one must not rest content with an ordinary degree of chastity, but should strive after an angelic purity, both of body and of mind.

§ III. *Instances of Covetousness.*—Lust cannot last without presents and money; thus, greed of gain is the offspring of lust. This is to be suppressed.

(1) By renouncing all unjust usurpation and whatever may savour thereof, and restoring what is ill-gotten. (2) By setting bounds to one's love of gain, even when lawful, lest, as St. Paul says, "*We fall into the snare of the devil.*" (3) If a Religious, by having naught that is his own, by giving, receiving, or lending nothing without leave. (4) By ridding oneself of costly, curious, rare objects, and of whatever savours of the world. (5) By not making use of more things than are needed, and of such only as are common, and are kept in a public place, not in one's room. (6) By avoiding bootless and dangerous thoughts and desires, "*which,*" as St. Paul bears witness, "*drown men in destruction and perdition.*"

§ IV. *Instances of Anger.*—Anger is the appetite for revenging injury or wrong. It is subdued, (1) By taking no vengeance, indeed, nor returning wilfully, or in intention, evil for evil. (2) By refraining, in the presence of him that has wronged us, from injurious and biting words, neither raising our voice in anger, nor lowering it out of sadness or aversion, nor refusing at seasonable times to speak to him by whom we have suffered; in his absence, not to complain of his deeds, or of himself, as being unjust, prejudiced, as favouring others, &c. In all these ways can we sin by anger. (3) By not nursing the remembrance of the injury received, nor indulge in thought that stir up indignation and strife; by setting aside the objections and answers wherewith the brain of an angered man is wont to teem.

§ V. *Instances of Melancholy and of Sloth.*—A quenched brand leaves a black coal behind; thus does anger, when lulled, leave the heart in sadness. Sadness, or melancholy, in its turn, begets sloth, or an aversion from spiritual and mental recollection. Now, a dissipated mind, finding no rest within itself, seeks it without. The remedy for this vice is as follows—(1) The conscience must be thoroughly searched, to discover whether it be in peace and security. Is it burdened with a grievous sin, or perplexed with the doubt thereof? Does the person feel any difficulty in laying bare his fault to his confessor, or in ridding himself of it? Is he troubled with fears and suspicions, which, while he keeps to himself, close his soul to the light from on high, a ray whereof would comfort him? Meanwhile, as he obstinately remains in darkness, his heart is overwhelmed with sorrow. For as a sprained joint gives unbearable pain, which cannot be assuaged by plasters, ointments, or any other external applications, so, from the sources detailed above, a more or less deep melancholy will spring, and such as will not yield to aught that is applied from without. Firstly, then, the Examen must be directed against concealing from the confessor aught that may concern the conscience. (2) Examine how deep a hold this melancholy has obtained on the heart. Has it caused an abscess—brought on a distaste for one's state, especially in the case of a Religious? Has it robbed us of our attachment to our Order, Superiors, and Rule? Do we obey readily, or with an effort? If this be our plight, we are dangerously seized, and still more so as we shrink from the remedy. For he that is thus affected abhors nothing so much as what would bring comfort to his soul. He solaces himself with what shuts out relief, such as murmuring and far-fetched reasons, which confirm him in his diseased fancies. Such a one must make his Particular Examen on the following points—

(1) To converse familiarly and affably with his inferiors; not to withdraw from the common recreation, nor to be gloomy in conversation. (2) To shut out from himself worldly business and diversions, and to keep at arm's length whatever may cause his heart to pour itself out to excess through the senses. Wherefore he will not go out of doors on purposeless errands, for unnecessary visits, even though they wear a semblance of piety. (3) He will keep from public amusements and gatherings, and, as far as possible, remain in his room. For one attacked with this disease has no taste for solitary occupations. Like as he who has lost all relish for wholesome food excites his appetite with condiments, which may tickle his palate, so should such a one beguile, by varying them, the monotony of solitary occupations, at one time reading, at another writing, or doing something else. (4) He shall flee, as he would the pestilence, friendly intercourse with seculars, nor allow himself to be entangled by busying himself with their affairs, their interests or concerns; since these can but deprive him of time and relish for the occupations of his state; for to relieve the monotony of these latter, as well as to hoodwink ourselves as to our indolent neglect of the duties of our state, we turn to what is foreign to our profession. (5) He shall not be a collector of news, nor lead the conversation to the

favours of fortune, the honours and delights of the world, for his languishing heart will be soon attracted by what he says or hears. (6) He shall divert his mind from such fancies, suppress all idle talk on such matters as deeds of daring, extraordinary good fortune, eminent posts and dignities, &c., for such befit rather those that are asleep than waking men. But especially shall he apply himself to his Spiritual Exercises, insisting not only on their exact fulfilment, but prolonging the time thereof, according to annotation thirteen among the twenty-one. In compliance with annotation six, he will most scrupulously observe the Additions, and earnestly strive to acquire devotion, which divine goodness will not fail to vouchsafe.

To sum up what has been said hitherto, he must be persuaded that the state of his soul is perilous and wretched, that without effort he will never rise therefrom, and that nothing aggravates this ailment so much as to indulge one's likings. The effort he has to make comprises these two things—(1) He must diminish and cut down his outward engagements, especially secular ones, restrain the wanderings of his senses, his going out of doors, bootless conversations, and thoughts which correspond therewith. (2) He must apply himself earnestly to his interior spiritual duties, nor rest content until he find a relish therein. He is not to attribute his dryness to God's proving of him, it being in nowise a trial but a punishment of his sloth and indifference. Outward occupations, undertaken according to the rules of well-ordered charity, are no hindrance to devotion and a spiritual relish; rather do these things afford each other mutual help and increase. The spirit of sloth, on the contrary, fleeing recollection, inordinately pours itself on the diversions and gratifications of sense, and by that very means aggravates its disease. The mind that revels in sensual pleasure, and is filled with the onions and leeks of Egypt, becomes dry, and cannot stomach the heavenly manna. It must further be noticed that it belongs to sadness of heart to hunt eagerly after earthly solace, and to be deeply attached thereunto when it has found it; wherefore, whoso is stricken with this disease must be weaned from these vile and abject gratifications, which so involve him in their meshes that he can hardly withdraw his foot from the snare. Besides, as one who nauseates bodily food, cannot keep what he takes on his stomach, the heat of which is diffused over the outward parts of the body, so it will be far worse with him that loathes spiritual sustenance if he allow the small degree of fervour which he possesses within him, which he should carefully husband, to escape through the wanderings of his senses.

§ 6. *Instances of Vanity and Pride.*—After the conquest of the afore-mentioned vices, it remains for us to attack pride and vanity, vices which, like the moth or gangrene, are inborn in man, and are the source of all evil; for they rob our best works of their merit, and blight the fair flowers of virtue. Vanity is the inordinate appetite of reputation, and of the praise of men. The glory that thus accrues to us being vain, this vice is called vainglory. Pride is the appetite of our own excellence which makes a man anxious to walk in things too great and too wonderful for him.

These vices find an incentive everywhere, even in what is contrary to them. They flourish on temporal and spiritual things, on good and bad actions, so far forth as reputation and distinction may be won thereby. The secular grows vain of his costly garb, the Religious of his threadbare habit. The former is proud of his well-appointed table, the latter of his abstinence and fastings; so much so that we have here an exception to the rule, that to weaken one vice is to weaken those that spring from it; for the conquest of other vices gives a fresh stimulus to vanity and pride, since, as we have said, both attach themselves to whatever is most sacred. The Examen on this matter may be arranged as follows—(1) Neither to aspire, or to strive after marks of honour. This was the vice of the Pharisees, of whom Christ said—*"They love the uppermost places at feasts, and the chief seats in the synagogues."** We have, therefore, to encounter an immense host, for ambition ever seeks the first place, at whatever age, in every condition, office, and place. (2) Let him not boast of his talents, if he has any, still less of those he has not; that is, let him avoid all occasions of boasting, where no other purpose can be served but that of making himself known. His life must be in accordance with that maxim of St. Bernard—"*Love to be unknown, and to be accounted as nothing.*" (3) He must avoid singularity, in his person, at table, and in his privacy, desiring to be forgotten of all, "*as a dead man out of mind.*" (4) He shall conform to the Community, nor allow himself any privilege or exemption necessity

* St. Matt. xxiii. 5.

does not require; and he will so yield to necessity as to put himself from time to time on a level with others. (5) He will speak neither of himself, nor of his concerns, but shall walk as if apart from himself. He shall behave and converse as if unmindful of himself, nor afford others an occasion of talking of him, for praise opens the first entrance to vainglory, and flattery the second. (6) He will not nurse thoughts of vanity by comparing or prefering himself to others. If he indulge such thoughts, he will be borne aloft like a feather and a thin bubble. (7) He will strive to weigh his gifts in a correct balance, referring to God what is good, and all the evil in him to himself.

The order here marked out is planned according to the nature and properties of the several vices; hence we must not conclude that it will be suitable for every one without distinction. For different persons are differently constituted. There is also a diversity of time and occasion. As in different individuals the same passions do not predominate, so even in the same person does the passion vary with the times, occasions, employments, and dispositions. Our enemy narrowly watches all these changes, in order to get our souls into his clutches. For, as St. Ignatius wisely observes—"*The enemy is wont to imitate a general who plans the seizure and plunder of a fortress. He first scrutinizes the site and strength of the place, and assaults it in its weakest point. Thus, too, does he prowl about the soul, and cunningly examine what virtues, whether theological or moral, it is provided with, or wanting in, and directs all his efforts, with the hope of undoing us, chiefly towards that point which he finds to be less pro-*

tected and guarded within us." This being the case, we must make the stoutest defence where the attack is the sharpest. The temptation we are most liable to will show on what our Examen should mostly be made. For the sake of greater clearness, we give further on a formula for choosing the subject of the Particular Examen according to the rules of election.

* Rule 14 of the first for the Discernment of Spirits.

CHAPTER XIV.

OF THE SUBJECT-MATTER OF THE PARTICULAR EXAMEN FOR SUCH AS ARE TROUBLED WITH NO VICE IN PARTICULAR.

THERE are some who aspire to or are advancing in the path of perfection, who are troubled with no vice in particular. This may arise from temperament, from natural goodness of character, or from the craft of the devil, who forbears to strike that he may make us heedless, and then trip us up unawares; or it may be that the passions slumber like wild beasts that have their fill, and behave as if they had departed from us. Wherefore, if you would discover which beast is the most troublesome and most formidable to you, you must attack it before it makes its onslaught on you. But with what can we begin our Examen when we are led to think that we have overcome and mastered a passion which slumbers, or is concealed by the wiles of the devil? What virtues are we to implant within us when our soul is undisturbed by rebellious passions?

To do this aright, it must be remembered that as in the way of perfection there are divers stages—beginners, proficients, and perfect—so the virtues proper to each of these degrees are different. In each of these degrees that virtue is to be chosen which is the most closely connected with others proper to the same state, so that by growth in one virtue you may increase in all the rest. Beginners, then, must apply themselves to the love of silence and solitude as to the fundamental virtue of their state. For as the first requisite for the cure of a bodily ailment is that the patient be removed to a good place, out of the way of disturbances which would hinder his recovery, so does our spiritual healing demand that, before all else, we keep our room, and be removed from the obstacles which make their way through our senses. Proficients must make their chief concern of humility and poverty of spirit, both of which virtues are, so to speak, the mother and the groundwork of all others proper to their state. The perfect should, by prayer and contemplation, deepen the union and familiarity of their souls with God. It must be kept in mind, that the name beginners comprises not only those who have just entered on the path of virtue, but all who are weak in virtue; and the name perfect does not depend on the number of years one may have professed virtue, but on the possession of solid virtue. For to numbers may we apply these words of the Apostle—"*Though for the time ye ought to be teachers, ye again have need that some one teach you the first elements of the oracles of God; and are become such as have need of milk, and not of solid food.*"* Let each one, then, enter into himself, and if he find he is wanting in the virtues of the very beginners, let him take rank amid babes and sucklings, and make his Examen according to the following rules.

* Heb. v. 12.

CHAPTER XV.

THE MATTER OF THE PARTICULAR EXAMEN FOR BEGINNERS.

HE will accustom himself to keep to his room; he will not leave it without a reasonable cause; never because he finds solitude and recollection irksome. Let him consider his reason for going abroad; his only motive must be the better service of God. This will he find in obedience to his Superior, and in charity to his neighbour. When these cease to detain him, he will return to his cell, as to his centre, as to the infirmary of his spiritual ailments, as to the workshop of virtue, wherein his soul is fashioned after God's image, as to a *bed of flowers*, where the soul may enjoy the embraces of God. The cell must be his first care, and the starting-point of his Examen; and as St. Bernard says (to the Monks of Mont-Dieu)—"Let goodwill be guided by the rule of obedience, and in its turn guide the body, teaching it to keep to one spot, to stay within the cell, and by itself; which, in a proficient, is the commencement of a good disposition, of favourable augury for the future. For it is impossible that a man should keep his soul fixed, who has not begun to keep his body perseveringly in one place."

2. From the love of the cell pass we on to the common life, striving might and main to conform to our brethren, which is to be prized above austerities

and peculiar devotions. We will rise, then, with the others, be the same to all, eat what they eat, and never take anything but what is set before them. Our prayer and recreation will be at the community hours, nor shall we shirk our share of the common offices and burdens. This will help to humble the heart, to break self-will (the main source of peril), to order all our doings aright, to deck the soul with a variety of virtues, to render one agreeable to all for that he is the same to all.

3. Having finished what regards common life, we proceed to private concerns. The times and hours for our several occupations must be fixed. This is not the place for treating of this distribution; still it is self-evident that important advantages depend on our doing our actions, not according to whim, but by rule, so that to-day may be the image of yesterday and of the morrow. Attention to this point gives peace of mind, saves time, bridles the license of the will, which it does not allow to be unruly. Although this may be more practical for those whose time and engagements are at their own disposal, nevertheless, it is even more so for those who, in these matters, are under the control of others. The former lay down a rule in conformity with their ordinary engagements, and keep it; the latter yield, so far as the duties imposed upon them by obedience are concerned, but when they have fulfilled these they return to the groove they have marked out. Unless this be done, a twofold loss ensues. (1) The precious moments intervening between a duty and a voluntary occupation are

wasted, which are of no less value than the filings and dust the goldsmiths so carefully sweep up in their workshops. (2) A diversity of occupations cannot but trouble a soul that is intent on many things. To restore its calm, it is of the greatest advantage to apply it at once to the ordinary occupations, from which necessity has summoned it. This care for order is not unlike the heavenly spheres which rule the universe by their harmoniously discordant movements. For though there does not appear to be so great a consonance between different parts, yet is this diversity most wisely established by the Prime Mover.

4. Next to the due ordering of our occupations comes that of our senses, and especially of the eyes, ears, and tongue.

The Eyes.

These require especial care, as they are exposed to greater danger. We should not fix our eyes on a woman, especially if she be still and do not observe us. David thus gazed at Bersabee and fell. We are to avoid sights, the image whereof easily impresses itself, but is difficult to efface. We must not be fond of looking at princely palaces and royal treasures. They are vanities, and darken the mind's perception of divine truth. Spurn as deadly poison novels, more or less unchaste and obscene pictures. Lastly, according to the rules of modesty laid down by St. Ignatius—"*The eyes should mostly be kept downcast, neither raising them without measure, or glancing with them around us.*"

The Hearing.

The ears must be closed to unseemly words, and it must be deemed an insult to utter such in our presence. Profane music is to be held in small account. We must be slow to listen to vain reports and to laughter-moving sayings, as they do not become us. Most true is what we read in the *Imitation of Christ*—"If thou withdraw thyself from superfluous talk and idle visits, as also from giving ear to news and reports, thou will find time sufficient and proper to employ thyself in good meditations. . . . If thou hadst not gone out, and listened to rumours, thou hadst kept thyself better in good peace; but since thou takest pleasure at times in hearing news, thou must bear with trouble of heart."*

The Tongue.

"*The tongue*," says St. James, "*is a restless mischief; it is full of deadly poison*," difficult to control and to keep subject to reason. Our first care, then, must be to curb it by the rule of silence, asking no questions unless when necessary, replying briefly if questioned. For he who speaks little to men will find more to say to God, and he who has accustomed himself to silence strikes off the head of a multitude of vices at one blow. But as the duty of our charge and brotherly love requires of us to speak, we must be careful lest necessary and useful speech degenerate into needless and harmful talk. We may make the Examen as follows on each of these defects.

* Book i., chap. 20.

Not to complain of any thing or person, be they many or few, neither in public nor in private, or to mention the fault of an absent person, or aught else that could offend him were he present. Not to flatter, lest we fall into a lie. To lie neither by excuse, in play, nor to any one's prejudice. Not to make use of ambiguous double-meaning words; for all duplicity and deceit is to be abominated. Not to adhere pertinaciously to one's opinions, a frequent source of strife and injurious words. Not to speak wrathfully, which is unpolite and wounds charity. Not to speak in a loud voice—the token of a dissipated mind. To avoid boasting—the offspring of pride. Not to reveal the secret intrusted, nor what should be kept secret, even though you be not forbidden to mention it. Not to fancy that he to whom you tell a secret will be more faithful in keeping it than yourself. Lastly, inasmuch as his condition allows, he will turn the conversation on God and on divine things, and await therefrom an abundant harvest of virtues.

Letters.

The faults of speech and of letter-writing are closely connected, but they are more pernicious in this latter case, as greater weight is attached to the written than to the spoken word, the former being more lasting than the latter. Let us be careful not to write anything inconsiderate in our letters, but to keep the rule laid down for us—"*In writing letters, not only must the rule 39 of the Summary be kept strictly, which prescribes that we are not to write without leave and without showing our letters to him the Superior shall appoint; but further, care must be taken that our letters contain not any mention of worldly or useless affairs, or which do not concern the writer. As, for instance, rumours, news about matters foreign to a Religious, certain forms of expression, or tropes and secular idioms,"* &c.

The Rules of Modesty.

Beginners must strive to regulate their exterior by these rules, shaping themselves thereby, as in a mirror, that their manners may be in conformity with the pattern of St. Ignatius set before his children after so many tears and prayers.

CHAPTER XVI.

THE MATTER OF THE PARTICULAR EXAMEN FOR PROFICIENTS.

IT belongs to proficients to choose a virtue for the matter of their Examen, and that virtue they have most need of, or which is the most contrary to the vice whereby they are most troubled. If they be not compelled by either of these causes, they may choose the virtue which is the foundation of the rest, or which most helps and disposes us to acquire them. We here take occasion to observe, that this Examen on virtues is to be made in an order wholly different from that on vice. With vices we begin with deeds, then pass on to words and thoughts. For, as we have said, the passion that breaks out into deeds is far more violent than one that passes not the boundaries of thoughts or speech. Wherefore, the greater evil has to be cured first, especially as the examination of what passes within the soul belongs to proficients, and not to mere beginners. Here we go on to a totally different plan. With these virtues the Examen must begin, and the conflict be opened with the inward acts thereof, and moreover, proficients are supposed to be more experienced in the discernment of their inward acts, and to have more light to perceive distinctly what is going on within them.

Further, there is no question but that inward acts are the very soul of virtue, while their outward mani-

-festations, unless duly referred to God, are as lifeless corpses, wholly incapable of begetting virtuous habits within us. For what fruit can we gain from a menial office, if it be not fulfilled out of humility? We meet with many who spend their whole lives in the vilest functions, without ever attaining humility. With what profit shall we submit to the rule of another, if the will to obey aright be wanting. Countless multitudes serve and spend their lives under the mastery of another, without making the least progress in the virtue of obedience. We must, then, make a beginning with inward acts, giving the first place to those from which, as from a stock, the other virtues branch forth, and that in the following order.

On Humility.

We may here apply what we have said above concerning pride, its contrary vice, besides which a fixed number of suitable acts, to be performed both in the morning and afternoon, is to be appointed, in the order which follows—(1) Turn the soul to the knowledge of self, to its poverty in virtue, the multitude of our sins, the smallness of our talents, and that the good we have comes not from us but from the mercy of God. (2) To desire that all may esteem me for what I really am, so that men may make of me as little as I deserve. Preparing myself inwardly to bear with the slights and other outward things that may occur. But here discretion must guide the mind, lest it go astray into vain fancies, or attempt what is above our strength, and so expose our virtue to shipwreck. (3) Mark that in others whereby they excel me, placing myself beneath them, and deeming them, in my inmost heart, my superiors. (4) To speak depreciatingly of myself, making little of what may fall to my lot, acknowledging my shortcomings. Here, too, is prudence needed, to guide us to the fitting time and place, and lest we fail in sincerity, or any affectation mingle itself with our words. (5) In that which regards our common intercourse, ever to yield to others the first place, as far as our condition allows: "*In giving honour, outdoing one another,*" as the Apostle says, and this not only in such homage which is seldom paid without insincerity, vanity, and outward demonstration, but in the functions and offices intrusted to us. (6) In the like spirit to take part now and then in the more menial offices of the house.

Poverty.

Here, too, may we apply what we said of covetousness. Moreover, this virtue is to be exercised a determinate number of times, in the following acts. We must examine ourselves as to our love and esteem for this virtue; our desire of experiencing its effects; how far we prefer to abstain from than to make use of things. He will consider that nothing allowed for his use is his own, and so be ready to be despoiled of them. He will look on whatever regards his diet, lodging, and clothing as an alms, and himself as a poor man, without any property. We are told of St. Francis Borgia that, on rising, he was wont to take his clothes as if they were a loan, which he returned in the evening when he undressed, and to have been of the same mind with regard to all other things allowed him for his use. Never are we to complain of the want of anything, but rather should we rejoice therein, as in an effect and experience of poverty. We will also prefer the more common things of the house to such as are more costly, for, as St. Aloysius was wont to say, poor folks like us, who live upon alms, should not even in thought aspire to what is of better quality, but be thankful if we get what is of a lower sort. To keep far from us, and from what we may have for our use, superfluities and valuables. To suffer at times the want of what is necessary, in order to be more like Christ and His Blessed Mother, whom we know to have frequently been in want of necessaries.

Obedience.

Let our hunger be to know the will of God in all things, and our meat its fulfilment. Let us behold God Himself in the person of the Superior, and close our eyes to all human considerations. Whatever we undertake let us do it from a motive of obedience, and submit only to God in obeying our Superior. We must rigorously exact from ourselves this satisfaction, that neither by the intercession of others, by complaints, by importunity, by show of sadness, or by tokens of coldness, will we ever make the Superior obey us. We will deem it a dangerous mischance if we stray from the path marked out by God. We will never propose ought against the orders given us but after prayer, and then with indifference and sincerity.

The observance of Rules.

The Rules embrace the subject-matter of nearly all the virtues. If you find yourself to violate any rule in particular, apply this Examen to it. It were also very useful to make it on our readiness to lay bare, in our account of conscience, whatever concerns the rules and our vows.

CHAPTER XVII.

THE MATTER OF THE PARTICULAR EXAMEN FOR THE PERFECT.

THE advantages of the particular Examen may be shared in even by the perfect, that is, by those who have reached such a stage of perfection as may be attained in this life. According to the light of Heaven shed abroad within them, they may take, as the matter of their Examen, first their outward or inward failings; then their punctuality in performing their spiritual duties at the appointed time, and in devoting thereto whatever leisure may be left to them by the occupations obedience or charity enjoin. Their next matter may be their care to improve still more in the performance of these exercises, and to draw therefrom a greater light; their interior recollection in the course of the day; how they keep themselves in God's presence. On the three theological virtues, faith, hope, and charity, fixing a certain number of acts to be made within a given time. On spiritual conversation, both at recreation and elsewhere, at home and abroad, according to the dispositions of those we may meet with, endeavouring everywhere to profit our neighbour. On the renewal of a right intention in all our works. On the ministries enjoined upon us, according to our Institute, whereby our neighbour is helped and made to draw near to God, an office most suitable to perfect men. How we acquit ourselves of them! Do we fulfil them as we ought? Do we turn aside to others less befitting our profession, to the detriment of the ministry committed to us? Do we readily and willingly spend ourselves on the poor and ignorant? With what zeal, or indolence, or gentleness? With what diligence or slackness? With what prudence and discretion, or with what hastiness and levity? These defects must be carefully searched out and noted down, that they may be reformed by this Examen.

We have given these several examples, suited to divers states, to show that matter will never be wanting. We now proceed to show how we may choose out of this abundance a particular subject better and more advantageous to our progress.

CHAPTER XVIII.

FORMULA OF CERTAIN MEDITATIONS HELPING ON THIS EXAMEN.

THOUGH we have treated at full length of the choice of the subject-matter of the Particular Examen, and it presents no difficulty to those who have been trained for a certain time in the use of these arms, and the Superior or ghostly Father can easily direct the inexperienced, yet, for the common advantage of both, we will set forth a meditation drawn up in accordance with the rules of election, to remove still further any chance of a mistake.

It is to be observed that we may here be met with a twofold doubt. (1) It may be asked whether one should not forthwith take up as the matter of his Examen a vice or a virtue, for in this world there is no man without some defect. Where it is evident that a vice, especially a gross one, predominates, there can be no question but that we must begin by combatting it before striving after virtue. (2) When we have selected the vice or virtue, as there are various methods of warring upon vice and of following after virtue, the question arises as to which of these means may be the best suited to my purpose. The following meditation will serve to clear up the first doubt.

Form of meditation for the choice of the matter of the Particular Examen.

The preparatory prayer as usual.

Prelude 1. I will consider my soul in the state wherein I am conscious of finding it, standing before God, the Searcher of hearts, and all His Saints, and anxious to know whether it be more pleasing to the Divine Majesty, and more profitable to itself, that I should in my Particular Examen endeavour to attain a certain virtue or to extirpate a certain vice.

Prelude 2. A prayer for the grace proper to this deliberation.

Point 1. I will set before me the passions and vices to which I am subject, from which I intend to select one for my Particular Examen. I will do the same with the virtues I desire to acquire, for the self-same purpose.

Point 2. I will consider three sets of men who have the knowledge of their vices. The first are lukewarm and remiss, and for all that they know their vices and wish to be rid of them, they always delay to apply the remedy. The second class are ready to take up arms against some of their failings, but not against that passion, or inclination, or habit they are unwilling to disturb, though this be the most pernicious, and the principal idol before which they bow down. The third class, being earnestly desirous to make progress, are ready to take any means of overcoming their vice, whatever it may be, for the glory of God and their soul's welfare. This point is merely an application of the meditation of St. Ignatius on the three classes of men.

Point 3. I will consider what vice or virtue within me has most need of the Particular Examen. To weigh this in a just balance, we may derive help from what has been said in the foregoing chapters. (1) If the vice is an occasion of offence or scandal, so as to lead others into sin. (2) If it have a large following, and be the root and source of other vices. (3) If it take its rise in a vehement passion or strong impulse, whereby we are carried away, so as to be liable to frequent falls. (4) If, taking into consideration the state I am in, the business I have to do, the persons I deal with, and the propensities I am conscious of, I feel myself more liable to fall into this sin than any other. (5) If the fault be an outward one, and hence more under the control of the will, and admitting more easily of this remedy, for if it be an inward failing the cure will become more difficult.

We may consider the virtues in like manner, in order to the selection of one of their number, examining which is more conformable with my vocation, or better suited to my engagements; which were a speedier remedy to the failing into which I relapse the oftenest, or would oppose the stoutest resistance to the passion to which I most frequently yield; which were more conducive to spiritual calm, more favourable to devotion, &c.

Point 4. Having pondered these circumstances, the next thing is to determine what vice or virtue preponderates, and is of greater importance, so as to choose for the subject-matter of the Particular Examen that which reason and our spiritual interests point out.

Point 5. Offer the election, when made, to God; beg grace to destroy this vice or to acquire this virtue. After war has been declared against a particular vice, then arises a question as to the best means of securing the victory. We will deal with it in the following meditations.

Form of meditation for uprooting a predominant vice, such as anger, for instance.

The preparatory prayer as usual.

Prelude 1. Imagine yourself to be like unto the leper, and to say—"*Lord, if Thou wilt, Thou canst make me clean;*"* or as the woman of Canaan, saying —"*Lord, my daughter is grievously afflicted with a devil;*"† or to blind Bartimæas, saying — "*Jesus, Master, have mercy on us.*"‡

Prelude 2. Ask light to know the remedy whereby we may overcome anger.

Point 1. Consider the turpitude of anger, how unseemly it is in a man, and especially in a Religious, and one, too, of the Society of Jesus, who is bound to labour for his own perfection and for the edification of his neighbour. How displeasing it is to God, to those who live with us, to those who are without. How much injury it has done to me and to others, and how much it has hindered my progress in virtue.

Point 2. Consider the beauty of meekness. Repre-

---

* St. Luke v. 12. † St. Matt. xv. 22. ‡ St. Luke xvii. 13.

sent it to thyself in the bearing of Christ, Who says—
"*Learn of Me, for I am meek and lowly in heart.*"*
Set it before thee as it was in the Saints, nay, even in thine own Fathers and Brethren whom thou hast known.

Point 3. Consider how often and how grievously thou hast been transported with anger. Look into the causes of thy falls. Do they arise from a bilious complexion, from habit, or over-quickness, or a want of thought, from pride, or pusillanimity, or from the liberty you allow yourself to blurt out whatever comes into your head.

Point 4. Consider the remedies thou hast applied, or heard of, or read; as, for instance, to hold thy peace, gentleness in action, to be so disposed that an insulting word will not provoke thee, to set aside the occupation which is to thee an occasion, to impress deeply on thy mind that wrongs can harm him that does them, and not the sufferer. Set Christ before Thyself, "*Who, when He suffered, He threatened not.*"† That it is the vice of brutes and not of men, for a man in anger divests himself of his manhood, and St. Basil calls it "*a passing madness.*" Think how often you have insulted God, and how patiently He has borne with you.

Point 5. Set before thee the end of thy creation, from the Fundamental Exercise and the Prelude for making an Election; also the special end of thy calling, which is God's greater glory, and the edification of thy neighbour. Having, then, set thy soul in calm and serenity, beg once more for a new outpouring of

* St. Matt. xi. 29.　† St. Peter ii. 23.

light divine, whereby to know and to choose what is meetest for the end aimed at.

Point 6. Setting aside all bias, and taking into consideration the inveteracy of the habit and other circumstances, ponder which of the means given above seems to be more effectual. Conclude the election, make an offering of it to God, that He may accept and establish it, as St. Ignatius prescribes.

This method may be adapted to any vice or evil habit whatsoever. For its more perfect use, it were well to consult the teaching of Cassian, who, in his fifth *Conference*, admirably sets forth the turpitude of the eight capital sins.

Formula for the extirpation of a fault of less importance, as, for instance, want of moderation in speech.

Preparatory prayer and preludes as heretofore.

Point 1. Consider, as was hinted above, how unseemly loquaciousness is in a Religious. The advantages of silence. How often this fault is committed. The causes of these falls, whether it be dissipation of mind, or the little account we make of the rules.

Point 2. The remedies of this fault. To set oneself a penance, or to ask the Superior to do so, whenever we fall into it. To bear in mind the maxim—"*In the multitude of words there wanteth not sin;*"* and what St. James says—"*If any man offend not in word, the same is a perfect man;*"† and, "*If any man among you thinketh that he is religious, and bridleth not his*

---

* Prov. x. 19.   † St. James iii. 2.

tongue, but deceiveth his heart, this man's religion is vain."* The esteem wherein the Saints held silence The loss of time for the chatterer and his hearers. How great a hindrance it is to prayer, to have our head filled with tales; and so forth, as in the former meditation.

The same formula may be applied to other faults.

To acquire a virtue the same road must be taken. Considering its beauty, advantages, the examples of Christ and His Saints. Contrasting it with the turpitude and pernicious results of the contrary vice. Applying the motives of election, as heretofore.

St. Ignatius, moreover, suggests another method, in the second mode of election, as—"What would I counsel one whose interest I have at heart?" "What would I wish to have done at the hour of death, at the Last Judgment?" A deliberation of greater importance may be spread over many days, taking one for the consideration of the reasons on one side; the next for those of the opposite side; a third for weighing both together; and lastly, after invoking the divine aid, completing the election in accordance with the dictates of prudence.

* St. James i. 26.

CHAPTER XIX.

THE END OF THIS EXAMEN.

THE end or purpose of this Examen is naught else but the performance of our good resolutions, the putting into practice our holy desires, and compliance with the divine inspirations. If we look well to it, in our other spiritual exercises we exert the memory that it may supply useful matter, the mind that it may reason thereupon, the will that it may assent thereto. But of what use is all this, if these thoughts, reasonings, and affections be not reduced to practice?

What good is there in planting and digging a vineyard, in surrounding it with a hedge, if the vines yield but leaves, and there be no wine to put into the cellar at vintage time? It is all the same if, when exercising the powers of the soul, and drawing forth what is in them, we fail to reduce our thoughts and purposes to practice. Now performance is the precise end of the Particular Examen, without which our unruly passions will behave like the labourers in the vineyard we read of in St. Matthew, who, at the time of the vintage, beat, stoned, and slew their master's messengers, and made no return to the owner of the vineyard.

The resolutions from which we expect fruit are of a twofold description. Some are directed to avoiding faults, others to the implanting or perfecting of virtue. Now the end of this exercise is to ensure the efficacy of both these classes of resolutions; for the Examen does away with our faults, be they voluntary or natural (that is, such as through our inclinations or passions lead us into moral delinquencies), and by frequent acts it implants habits of virtue. So that the Particular Examen may well be deemed a universal instrument for perfecting the soul, both within and without, in the sight of God and of man. Other fruits peculiar to this exercise follow on these two main results. The conflict with vice leads us to that self-knowledge so highly prized and earnestly sought for by all who tend to perfection. Experience and practice render visible and tangible the great difference existing between the time when we make our resolution and that when we are unfaithful to it, between those motions stirred up within us by the bountiful hand of God's mercy, and those which well up from our natural corruption and inborn frailty. In time of prayer, under the sense of God's presence, the mind is conscious of being enlightened with holy thoughts, the will kindles with pious desires and affections. On the other hand, when prayer is over, we find ourselves to be quite different. The mind is then darkened, nay, even blind, to heavenly things. Vain, idle thoughts, grovelling in what makes for our ease and gratification, now well up from the heart, the will wavers under the shock of our perverted lusts. Like as water when taken off the fire resumes its wonted temperature, so does the spirit, unsustained by prayer, return to its remissness and love of creatures. This is how we so soon fall short of our morning resolution. He, then, that turns his attention to these resolutions and their frequent violations, soon learns to distinguish between the divine and his own spirit, between the motions of nature and those of grace. He finds himself to be like an infant, who, so long as he is upheld by his nurse, is able to stand up, but, not having strength enough to go alone, he falls down as soon as this support fails him. In our ministrations to our neighbour we will learn to regard ourselves as a page bearing a message from his Prince, whose only business is to fulfil the commission he is intrusted withal. If the words of the page have any effect on his hearer, it is to be attributed to him that sent him, not to himself. Thus, too, shall we acknowledge the hand of God in the fruit we may chance to produce either in ourselves or our neighbour, and ascribe whatever we may effect to the Source of all good. Blind, indeed, to all self-knowledge must he be, and barren will his labours, both for himself and for others, prove, who presumes to attribute to himself the fruit of his efforts in any case; for if this fruit be remarkable and noteworthy, its very excellence proclaims its source. We cannot but be fully convinced that such results are due to a cause far higher than ourselves when, by the daily examen, we are made to see how little we effect where we strive the most, how easily we fall when most sure of ourselves. Such an experience must bring down and root out our pride and presumption. Like as when we see a man, whose poverty is well known to us, going forth in costly array, we infer that he has either borrowed or stolen it, so, too, one who is aware of his infirmity will not attribute it to himself, if he chance to gain some precious advantage for his own, on his neighbour's behoof. Now this is the priceless fruit to be derived from this Examen, so far forth as it is concerned with our defects.

But of no less excellence are its fruits, if we consider it as a means for acquiring virtue. It enriches and decks the soul, as it were, in brocaded vesture. As virtues are engendered by repeated acts, by the mortifications of the contrary passions and vices, this practice must needs implant solid, firmly-rooted habits. Now habit implies facility; solid virtue implies somewhat more than a mere seeming, a weakly counterfeit, bolstered up by the fervour of devotion when it is present (and thus without substance or durability); it implies virtue, forged on the anvil of mortification, shaped by repeated victories over the contrary vice. From virtues such as these are begotten robust health, lasting peace, purity of aims. With them the passions lay down their arms and yield subjection to reason, which is given to man to hold his passions in check, to direct his actions, and which can never be brought so low by vice as to be subject to it, or so shackled by evil habits as not to struggle against them. This is the cause of the unrest of the wicked, for whom, as the Scripture says, there is no peace, while the just revel in the abundance thereof.

From this there arise a relish and pleasure in action which ensure perseverance. When the stomach rejects wholesome and choice food, it is a sign of its being charged with an evil humour, that takes away the appetite. When medicine has purged it away, not only will the stomach not reject this food, but the palate will be tickled. The like happens in the practice of virtue. Virtue is for all men a most wholesome and savoury aliment; yet to beginners, whose spiritual taste is depraved by passions, vices, and evil habits, it seems insipid and bitter. But the peccant humour having yielded to the practice of contrary acts, as virtue is, in very deed, most conformable to our reasonable nature, the soul delights in this food, which then becomes sweeter to its palate than *honey and the honeycomb*.

It must not, however, be disguised that this exercise lays us open to two temptations of opposite tendencies, yet, while giving occasion to them, it fails not to supply a remedy. For if the knowledge of our vileness is apt to engender pusillanimity and distrust, the practice of virtue may produce self-reliance and vanity. From this very self-confidence—in a way, too, the ailing person himself cannot account for—there proceeds such pusillanimity and faint-heartedness as to withdraw the soul from its undertakings, and to make it take refuge in its former carelessness. The task we have set about being far beyond our powers, the soul, if she rely thereon, will forthwith discover that she cannot with her ten thousand hold her ground against a foe coming against her with twenty thousand; wherefore, despairing of the victory, she makes terms, and relapses into the shameful slavery of her vices and passions. The remedy for both temptations is contained in this very exercise. The practice thereof consists in making a resolution in the morning to watch over ourselves during the course of the day, to take note of and to count our falls, and to renew at the same time our good purposes. He who thus looks to himself and takes account of his failings, conscious as he is of his weakness, expects to fall, and when that comes to pass, he is not disheartened or discouraged at what he foresaw when entering upon the conflict. By renewing his resolution after a fall he is far from yielding to discouragement, by the very fact of his repeating his resolve. Nor will he rely too much on his own strength, since he finds that he stumbles, in despite of his will and resolution to the contrary. Whence we may see the wondrous efficacy of this remedy and the wisdom of the physician, who, by means of such easy and simple methods,' wages war so successfully on vice and gathers such store of virtue, showing, too, how to blend confidence with distrust, so as to steer clear of the two extremes of faint-heartedness and vanity.

CHAPTER XX.

FOR WHOM IS THIS EXAMEN SUITED?

FROM what we have said of the matter, plan, and purpose of the Examen, it is easy to determine what persons may find their profit in making use of it. It is suited to all who aspire to spiritual progress—to beginners, proficients, the perfect, to such as are engaged in occupations with their neighbours, to those who enjoy a pious leisure, to the talented, and to such as are more sparingly gifted; its end being to uproot vice and implant virtue, to ground the soul in self-knowledge and self-diffidence, to beget within it trust in God, and that purity of heart, real peace, which is founded upon the subjection of our appetites and passions, and in conformity with right reason. If there be any one who has no need of pursuing this end, either wholly, or in part, he may be excused from making this Examen. But as there are none such, so may no one who has the slightest care for his spiritual progress claim to be exempted.

Two pleas are usually urged, or can at least be invented. The first takes its stand upon the method. It may be said that, beyond a question, every exercise is not suited to every one. For others, this method is too minute and refined—for some, nay, for many. Does not St. Ignatius himself expressly teach in his *prescriptions for making election*, that among those who are not deficient in mental abilities, every one has not the requisite dispositions, and that hence they should be dispensed from those exercises of contemplation and union with God, which presuppose extraordinary mortification and purity? Granting all this, we deny its applicability to the Particular Examen. For this exercise is of such a nature as to make no great demands on our intellect or capacities. Its sole requirement as to the will is an honest desire of progress. See the 18th and 19th Annotations of St. Ignatius.

The other plea for exemption is taken from the subject-matter. Some there are who, either from natural goodness of character, or from the failing of occasions, the fervour of passing devotion, or their former earnestness in mortifying themselves, are not conscious of any uprising of passion or temptation which gives them much trouble, so that they find not any enemy to attack. This stratagem is big with the most grievous perils. We have known men who in their novitiate, and the years immediately following it, might have been likened to Angels, but who, on being exposed to occasions, have fallen headlong into anger, envy, ambition, carnal passions, and have gone so far as to apostatize from Religion, and go over to the enemy. What can we assign as the cause of such a disaster, if it be not their negligence in waging war with their secret passions, which as we heretofore observed, conceal themselves, and lurk within them, awaiting their opportunity for striking a fatal blow.

It must, therefore, be taken as certain, that whatever the natural goodness of character may be, unless it be singularly favoured by divine grace and sustained by mortification, it is not to be trusted. For, as St. Bernard says, "Whether thou like it, or no, the Jebusite dwells within thy borders, nor can he be driven forth, but only kept under."* In other words, savage beasts make their lair in an honest and good heart, that seems naturally formed for virtue, and although they slumber awhile as if they were dead, yet are they alive, and will show it when occasion serves. Thus, if another has better success in his studies, the stings of envy make themselves to be felt. An order is given which is not so agreeable, the will kicks against it, and we feel an aversion for the Superior, as if he were unkind in his treatment of us. Now these feelings, and countless others of the same kind, if not worse, what do they prove, but that passions as yet unsubdued have their abode within us; so that Cassian had the greatest reason for saying, "Whatever the vices we have brought with us into solitude without having remedied them, they will be found to lurk within us, instead of being made away. For if solitude can open unto such as have amended their conduct the way to the loftiest contemplation, and unfold the knowledge of heavenly mysteries into their purified gaze, so is it wont not only to preserve, but to increase the vices of those who are not wholly reformed. One may deem himself meek and humble so long as he is separated from human intercourse, but such a one will soon fall back into his former state when any disturbance chances to befall. His vices then forthwith raise their heads, and like unbroken horses whom long repose has rendered unmanageable, they rush forth from their lurking-places, to the destruction of

* *Sermon* lviii. *on the Canticles.*

their driver. For our vices, unless amended, become more violent by the breaking off of intercourse with our fellows. That shadow of patience we fancied ourselves to possess while mingling with our brethren, and which we maintained out of respect for them, the fear of disgrace, is lost in the lull of a deceitful security. We might as well say that venomous reptiles or wild beasts, in the solitude of their lairs, are harmless, because they injure no one. Their harmlessness is the effect of solitude, not of natural goodness. Wherefore the absence of our fellow-men who might provoke us to anger is of little use for our perfection, for unless we have not already trained ourselves to patience, our anger will burst forth at inanimate objects and the merest trifles."* Cassian thus teaches, and that with great truth, that it is of the utmost importance for us to be diligent in repressing our secret passions. Unless this be done, although we may be secured against temptations from without, we cannot promise ourselves any safety. Now this is just what is most effectually done by means of the Particular Examen.

Some may, perhaps, deem their passions to be already sufficiently mortified in their inward motions, and that they may on that account dispense with this Examen. But let them hearken to St. Bernard—"Who is there that has completely cut off from himself all that is superfluous, as not to need the pruning-knife any more? Believe me, what has been pruned down, puts forth new shoots; what has been put to flight, returns; what we have quenched, kindles

* *Of the Institute of Cœnobites*, book viii., chap. xvii.

afresh; what is slumbering, awakens again. It avails little to have pruned once, we must do it often; if possible, always. For unless you delude yourselves, you will never find matter wanting for the pruning-knife."

Nothing could be more truly said; and granting there are no vices to mow down, are there no virtues to be gathered in and fostered? St. Ignatius, though he attained to so sublime a height of sanctity, kept to the Particular Examen, as to the trusty helpmate and most efficacious means of his perfection, till his dying day. There may arise a question as to the time of making it. If we consult the Constitutions, Rules, and the Book of the Exercises, we shall ascertain two points. (1) That we are to examine our consciences twice a day, as is ordered in the Institutions.* The Fourth General Congregation or Chapter, in its sixth canon, decrees that the times of these examens per day is to be strictly kept to. This, also, is our invariable practice. (2) As regards the Particular Examen, St. Ignatius, as we have seen, teaches most expressly, that it is to be made at noon and in the evening. Since, then, two special times are appointed for the general and Particular Examen, it is most advisable to make both together, and never to omit them, even though we may be necessitated, now and then, by our occupations to change the usual hour.

* Part iv., chap. iv., sec. 3.

APPENDIX.

From Father Nepveu's "Spirit of Christianity."

DEFECTS CONTRARY TO HUMILITY.[*]

WE cannot know well the nature of humility, without knowing the defects which are opposed to it: nor can we acquire this virtue except by labouring earnestly to remedy those defects, which ought to be the subject of our examinations of conscience. These defects are—

First, self-complacency upon our good qualities, whether of body or mind, whether natural or supernatural; also an excess of thought concerning our good qualities, and a lack of effort to prevent the movements of vanity that spring therefrom.

Second, speaking too easily of one's self and of things favourable to one's self, or of that which can give occasion to others to notice or to speak of us.

Third, to prefer one's self mentally to others, whether for virtue or for talents, and to consider voluntarily their defects rather than their good qualities; also to act in a contrary manner concerning ourselves.

[*] Treatise ii., ch. vi.

Fourth, to feel chagrined at hearing others praised, and to try cunningly to hinder their being so highly esteemed.

Fifth, to excuse one's self always when blamed, to refuse to recognize one's faults, or to avow that one has been in the wrong.

Sixth, to have a certain air of self-sufficiency and superiority in conversation, and a contempt for others and their opinions, also to wish always to take the lead.

Seventh, to dispute with an obstinate attachment to one's own opinion, to prefer one's opinion always to that of others, persuading one's self that he has light on the matter which others have not.

Eighth, to allow one's self to be too much dazzled by high employments, by great successes, by honours, by reputation, and by making too much account of all these things, instead of regarding them with fear or pity like a truly humble soul.

Ninth, to feel too much chagrined when our enterprises do not succeed, even those undertaken for the glory of God or the salvation of our neighbour; for this often proceeds less from our zeal than from a secret pride which makes us fear that the lack of success may draw blame or contempt upon us.

Tenth, to feel bitterly or coldly towards persons who appear not to esteem us so highly as we think we deserve; to revenge their contempt by despising them, or giving way to a malignant joy when others appear to despise them or speak disparagingly of them.

Eleventh, to speak too easily or without real

necessity of the defects of others, from a feeling of secret jealousy or a desire that we may be preferred to them.

Twelfth, to wish that others should know and remark our good qualities and good works, and to do them with the view of meriting thereby their esteem and approbation.

Thirteenth, to perform more willingly works of supererogation than of obligation, because they distinguish us and flatter our vanity and satisfy our self-love.

Fourteenth, to do more willingly a good work which is apparent and gives fame than that which is known to God alone; also to have no care to refer all that we do and all the praises our actions draw upon us, to God, instead of saying with the Psalmist—"*Not to us, O Lord, not to us, but to Thy name give glory.*"

Fifteenth, to desire perfection and all virtues and spiritual gifts more for love of our own excellence than with a view to the glory of God.

DEFECTS CONTRARY TO MEEKNESS.*

First, to cherish resentment against persons whom we believe to have offended us; to talk of them willingly in a spirit of bitterness, to desire to revenge ourselves upon them, and to seek the occasions and the means thereof.

* Treatise v., ch. v.

Second, to abandon one's self to choler concerning those who have displeased or affronted us.

Third, to manifest one's resentment either by offensive language, or by violent actions.

Fourth, to blame too severely those whose faults we are obliged to correct, or to complain too sharply when we have occasion to be dissatisfied.

Fifth, to look on the faults of others rather with indignation than with pity, and to be little disposed either to accept their excuses or to pardon their shortcomings.

Sixth, to reprehend the failings of others with too much warmth, or with bitterness, or with pride.

Seventh, to punish beyond what the offender deserves; for meekness would always make the punishment less than the offence.

Eighth, to sustain our opinions with too much warmth or stubbornness, and with contempt of those of other people.

Ninth, to treat others uncivilly or with bluntness or haughtiness.

Tenth, to refuse harshly or indifferently those things which we can easily grant.

Eleventh, to fail to express our sorrow when we cannot reasonably accede to the demands of others, and to soften the rigour of refusal by kindliness of manner.

VARIOUS ACTS OF CONTEMPT OF THE WORLD.*

Firstly, we must have an interior contempt for all external show, and all that has the appearance of grandeur, as being opposed to the state of Jesus Christ, which is one of humility and self-annihilation.

Secondly, we must, on the contrary, have a great esteem and respect for everything like poverty and humiliation—for poor people and poor dwellings, &c., because all such matters are more in harmony with the poor and humble state of our Blessed Lord.

Thirdly, we must neither seek the favour nor the friendship of the great; we must be more willing to converse with the poor than the rich, and to labour for their salvation; because there is less danger in labouring for the humble than for the great; and there is a greater profit in it, and more ease in approaching them.

Fourthly, we must not push ourselves into affairs that may attract especial public attention, even under the pretext of zeal—unless, perchance, we may be urged thereto by the glory of God, by charity or by obedience.

Fifthly, when we are obliged to take part in such affairs, we must endeavour to perform the most painful and least honourable portion of the service; and to act so that the success of the enterprise may be attributed to others rather than to ourselves.

Sixthly, we must speak as little as possible of ourselves, never speaking to our own advantage

---

* Treatise vii., ch. vi.

or reporting any good act that we may have performed — except we are compelled to do so by necessity, or by considerations for the edification of our neighbour.

Seventhly, we must never do good before men, neither to please them, nor to obtain their approbation, for we must only aim at pleasing God.

Eighthly, we must take care not to make much of our good actions, lest we should vitiate our good intentions, and self-love, caprice, and the wish to please men should mix themselves up in our best actions, rendering them hateful in the sight of God: and when even we may have done all that we ought (and who would dare to flatter himself that he had done his whole duty?), we must believe ourselves, according to our Lord's counsels, useless servants.

Ninthly, we must always be more willing to do good secretly than openly.

Tenthly, we must be perfectly content with the few talents that God has given us, and with the little success that may attend our efforts—persuaded that we may often glorify God more worthily by humbly accepting our abjection than by obtaining the most splendid successes, which might make us vain and proud.

Eleventhly, we must, as far as possible, avoid the praise of men—we must fear it much, and receive it with pain and confusion, bearing in mind that the applause of the world is not the only recompense of our good actions, and taking heed lest it make us lose our eternal reward. We must remember that the commendation of the world, if we seek it or rest contented with it, only draws upon us the condemnation of God.

Twelfthly, when God favours us with any success, the greater it is, the more we must humiliate ourselves before God, and stand abashed to think that God, to manifest His power, condescends to use such weak instruments as ourselves; and we must refer all the glory to God, without reserve, remembering the word of our Lord to His disciples—"*Rejoice not in this that spirits are subject unto you.*"* We must not rejoice in the success obtained, but rather in the hope that our names are written in Heaven.

Thirteenthly, when we are humiliated and despised by our fellow-men, so far ought we to be from feeling afflicted and discouraged, that we should rejoice in it and love our abject condition, because we may be led through it into a state of conformity with our humiliated and suffering Saviour.

VARIOUS ACTS OF MORTIFICATION.†

I. To moderate our natural activity and zeal, even in regard to our best undertakings.

II. To relinquish any useless project, to the execution of *which we feel* strongly inclined; and to suspend our action, in case of a good and useful one, so that we may act from a fixed principle, rather than from a natural enthusiasm.

III. To deprive ourselves of some gratification, or

---

* St. Luke x. 20.   † Treatise viii. ch. vi.

of the satisfaction of curiosity concerning anything whatever, after the example of St. Francis Borgia, who, being very fond of hawking, often, from a spirit of mortification, deprived himself of the innocent pleasure of seeing the hawk seize his prey, by closing his eyes at the moment; in which action he imitated David, that great Saint and King, who overcome with thirst, mortified himself, and made a sacrifice to the Lord by pouring out upon the ground the water which had been obtained for him with great labour and danger.

IV. To restrain our anxiety to hear the news, and the common rumours of the day, particularly if they affect the good name of our neighbours.

V. To guard our eyes carefully, never allowing them to rest upon any dangerous or impure object.

VI. Not to indulge in raillery in conversation, however harmless or agreeable it may be—particularly with persons with whom we are not on perfectly good terms.

VII. To withhold at times a witticism which might raise our own reputation, and please the hearers, particularly if it would be uncharitable, or might encourage our vanity.

VIII. To behave kindly and politely towards those whom we dislike, or who have used us ill; and not to avoid meeting them.

IX. To avoid making complaints to persons in whom we confide, that we may relieve our hearts of their burden.

X. Not to complain of our food when it is not entirely to our liking, remembering that it is not,

Appendix. 141

after all, so bad as the gall which our Blessed Lord took for love of us: and to complain, when it is unavoidably necessary, without bitterness or anger.

XI. Not to seek delicate food, not to eat with avidity, and to shun all sensuality in our eating: mortifying ourselves always in something, particularly in food that may be hurtful to us.

XII. To abstain from the reading of all dangerous books, of those which will only satisfy a vain curiosity, and especially of those which may excite the passions.

XIII. To abandon entirely all dangerous pleasures, and to moderate those that are innocent, abstaining from them at times for a penance and mortification.

XIV. Never to seek, and sometimes even to avoid agreeable odours, concerts of music, and all that can flatter the senses and enervate the heart.

XV. Never to occupy ourselves with vain and useless thoughts, although they may be harmless in themselves; and to endeavour as much as possible to restrain the wanderings of our imagination.

XVI. To follow with fidelity the rule of life prescribed by our director, and never to dispense with the observance of it, from our own inconstancy, or from weariness.

XVII. To quit whatever we may be engaged in, as soon as the time shall come for our religious exercises; that is, when we can do so without wronging any other person, or behaving uncharitably.

XVIII. To moderate our solicitude concerning ourselves, and our extreme sensibility to petty ills, which makes us complain without a cause and like to be pitied.

XIX. Not to be too strongly attached to anything that gives us great pleasure, but to try to disengage our mind and heart from it, and by turning towards God, to renounce it altogether.

XX. To repress our propensity to talkativeness, to speak little, and that without haste or too much warmth.

XXI. To perform certain regular penances, and never to omit them without good reason and by the advice of our director.

XXII. Never to place ourselves in immodest postures, though they may be comfortable.

XXIII. Never to reprove any person when we feel at all moved, but to wait till we are perfectly calm.

XXIV. To keep silence in our trials, and not to seek for consolations with too much anxiety and earnestness.

XXV. Never to excuse ourselves unless we are obliged to by considerations of obedience, or of charity, or of edification of our neighbour.

Although the most of the things composing this practice of self-denial are very easy and light, yet it is undeniably true, by experience, that a soul which is faithfully exercised in it will surely arrive in a short time at a high state of perfection : because this exercise accustoms a person by degrees to overcome his caprices and to die to himself, and establishes in the heart, upon the ruins of selfishness, a perfect love of God.

www.ingramcontent.com/pod-product-compliance
Lightning Source LLC
Chambersburg PA
CBHW030319170426
43202CB00009B/1072